Susan,
- Since you own
3 of these I figure
you should something
about them.
Love
Dad.

Howell Book House
A Simon & Schuster Macmillan Company
1633 Broadway
New York, NY 10019

MACMILLAN is a registered trademark of Macmillan, Inc.

Library of Congress Cataloging-in-Publication Data
Commings, Karen.
The shorthaired cat : an owner's guide to a happy, healthy pet / Karen Commings.
p. cm.
Includes bibliographical references.

ISBN 0-87605-475-0

1. Cats. I. Title.
SF447.C65 1996
636.8'2—dc20   95-53973
          CIP

Manufactured in the United States of America
10 9 8 7 6 5 4 3 2 1

Series Director: Dominique DeVito
Series Assistant Directors: Ariel Cannon and Sarah Storey
Book Design: Michele Laseau
Cover Design: Iris Jeromnimon
Illustration: Jeff Yesh
Photography:
  Cover Photos by Scott McKiernan/Zuma
  Mary Bloom: 52,109, 129
  Paulette Braun/Pets by Paulette: 6, 62, 67, 75, 83, 90, 142, 144
  Paul Butler: 20, 21, 22, 28, 34, 38, 39, 40, 84, 137
  Chanan: 23, 24, 25, 26, 27, 28, 29, 30, 31, 32, 33, 36, 37, 40, 140
  Scott McKiernan/Zuma: 11, 12, 14, 19, 36, 46, 58, 78, 81, 92, 120, 133
  Renée Stockdale: 26, 35, 43, 53, 71, 88, 89, 97, 104, 122, 125, 134
  Judith Strom: 10, 42, 68
  Jean Wentworth: 5, 7, 8, 14, 15 ,44, 45, 57, 60, 61, 66, 79, 107, 110, 111, 113, 114, 118, 121, 139, 145
  Karrin Winter/Dale Churchill: 38
  Photo on page 17 courtesy of Socks the Cat Fun Club.
  Photo on page 16 courtesy of 9-Lives.
Production Team: Troy Barnes, Trudy Brown, John Carroll, Jama Carter, Kathleen Caulfield, Trudy Coler, Amy DeAngelis, Matt Hannafin, Vic Peterson, Terri Sheehan and Marvin Van Tiem III.

Contents

part one

Welcome to the World of Shorthaired Cats

1 The World of Shorthaired Cats 5
2 The Domestic Shorthair 12
3 The Shorthaired Breeds 19
4 Your Individual Cat 42

part two

Living with Your Shorthaired Cat

5 Your Cat and Your Home 52
6 Feeding Your Cat 66
7 Grooming Your Shorthaired Cat 78
8 Your Cat's Physical Health 88
9 Your Cat's Mental Health 107

part three

Enjoying Your Cat

10 Your Cat's Behavior 118
11 Training Your Cat 133
12 Having Fun with Your Cat 139

part four

Beyond the Basics

13 Additional Reading 148
14 Resources 152

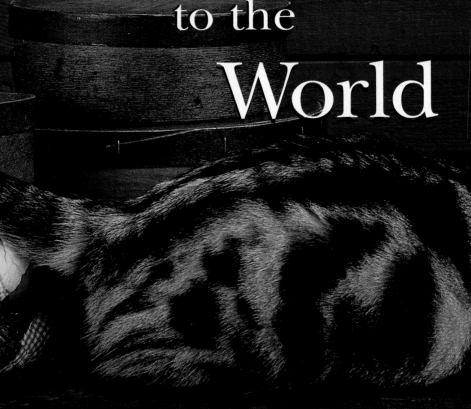

Welcome

to the
World

of
Shorthaired
Cats

External Features of the Shorthaired Cat

chapter 1

The
World of
Shorthaired
Cats

Welcome to the world of cats. As a new cat owner, you will be sharing your life and your home with one of America's most popular pets. Given proper care and attention, your cat will provide you with companionship and love, be sensitive to your moods and emotional states and add the spark of enjoyment to your life that living with a pet provides.

Not only do cats make wonderful companions, but studies have shown that having a cat provides many

*Over the
centuries, cats
have been treated
like royalty and
also despised by
humans.*

health benefits as well. Simply stroking your cat can help you overcome stress, reduce blood pressure and heart rate, and lower your risk of heart attack. Listening to your cat purr has the same effect as many relaxation techniques.

Cats are animals of opposites: free-spirited and capable of reverting to their wild instincts, yet dependent on us as caregivers to provide them with food, shelter and love to reach their full potential. They are capable of giving you extra comfort when you are ill and yet can completely ignore you when you are healthy. They are mysterious, at times seeming to be deeply lost in thought, and at other times so obvious in letting you know what they want. Cats are fascinating creatures with rich emotional and behavioral lives. We have only recently begun to understand them as a species, and the body of that knowledge and understanding is increasing every day. So, sit back and take a tour through the wonderful world of cats.

The First Cats

Man's relationship with the domestic cat has been relatively short in evolutionary terms. Dogs, goats, pigs and cattle were first domesticated when early man began to settle and turn to agriculture ten to twelve thousand years ago. The first domestic cats did not appear until between 3000 and 4000 B.C. when the ancient Egyptians began settling in the Nile Valley.

Most researchers believe the ancestor of the domestic cat to be a small, sandy-colored desert dweller with a lightly spotted coat called the African wild cat (*Felis libyca*). Slightly larger than today's domestic cat, this docile, easily tamed African wild cat is known to inhabit northern Africa and parts of India and Asia. Its larger size conforms to the sizes of the mummified cats found in Egyptian tombs. The African wild cat's natural habitat corresponds to the areas man inhabited in northern Africa when record of the first domestic cat appeared.

> ## AND THE WORD WAS "CAT"
>
> In addition to archaeological evidence, there is etymological evidence that the domestic cat originated in ancient Egypt. The English word "cat," the French "chat," the German "Katze," the Spanish and Syrian "gato," the Byzantine "katos," the Latin "catus" or "cattus," and the Arabic "qitt" or "quttah," are derived from the Nubian word "kadiz," meaning cat. Nubia is a desert region and ancient kingdom in the Nile Valley that included southern Egypt.

Cats are fascinating creatures with rich emotional and behavioral lives.

Contributing to the evolution of today's housecat was another African cat called the jungle cat (*Felis chaus*), also believed to have been kept by the ancient

Egyptians. Like the African wild cat, the jungle cat is sandy-colored, but it has ticked tabby markings.

The Egyptians had a close religious relationship with animals, and the cat was no exception. Animals were thought to share part of their existence with the gods, and through them, the Egyptians could contact the divine. The cat came to be associated with the goddess Bastet, daughter of the sun-god Ra, who protected Ra and ensured his continued well-being. Burials of mummified cats were part of rituals performed in her honor.

References to cats in ancient Greece appear frequently although not as often as in Egypt. Cats appear in Aesop's fables from the 6th century B.C., in Callimachus's "History of the Animals" from the 5th century B.C. and in "Dialogue of the Syracusans," written by Theocritus in the 3rd century B.C.

HEMINGWAY'S CATS

Writer Ernest Hemingway was a cat lover who kept up to fifty or more felines at his home in Key West, Florida. Many of the cats who lived with Hemingway were polydactyls, or cats with six or more toes. Hemingway's first polydactyl cat was given to him by a ship's captain. Today, descendants of the original Hemingway cats live the life of luxury at the Ernest Hemingway House and Museum in Key West. Many of the cats bear the names of famous writers and movie stars—Gertrude Stein, Edgar Allan Poe, Liz Taylor, Ginger Rogers—a tradition that was established by Hemingway himself.

The European wildcat (Felis silveris) *may have been the species that introduced the dark tabby pattern found in domestic cats like this one.*

The domestic cat spread through Europe and Britain with the Romans, who brought it from Egypt. During its spread throughout Europe, as well as Asia, the

Egyptian cat mated with other small cat species; these matings, over the centuries, produced the domestic cat that we know today. Although the cat's two African ancestors have subdued tabby markings, the European wild cat (*Felis silvestris*) may have been the species that introduced the genes for the dark tabby pattern found in the contemporary feline.

The domestic cat's relationship with humans has not always been a pleasant one. Throughout its history, the cat has been both revered and hated. The sacred status that the cat held in ancient Egypt was lost during the Middle Ages, when it became associated with evil, sorcery and witchcraft. Cats, especially black ones, were thought to be incarnations of the devil. As a result, tens of thousands of cats, along with their mostly female owners, were persecuted and killed as part of religious rituals.

In the fourteenth century, bubonic plague, a disease carried by rats, ravaged Europe and Asia, killing more than seventy-five million people. Because of their part in helping eliminate the plague-carrying rodents, cats once again gained favor in the eyes of man.

The First American Cats

Having secured a reputation as mousers, cats traveled to America on ships with the first settlers from Europe and Britain. Recently, researchers have studied various feline traits such as

---

AILUROPHILES

People who love cats are called ailurophiles. Over the centuries, the grace and beauty of the cat have been an inspiration to statesmen, religious leaders, authors and artists. The prophet Muhammad was very fond of cats. His cat, Muezza, used to curl up in the sleeve of his robe. Legend says that, on one occasion when he had to go out, Muhammad cut off the sleeve of his robe rather than disturb his sleeping cat. And left-handed scientist Albert Einstein often wrote with his right hand so as not to disturb his cat, Sizi, who often slept on his left arm.

Some of history's famous ailurophiles include:

ROYALTY AND STATESMEN:
Queen Victoria
Abraham Lincoln
Vladimir Lenin
Calvin Coolidge
Theodore Roosevelt

WRITERS:
Petrarch
Victor Hugo
Charles Dickens
Colette
Mark Twain
A. A. Milne
Henry James
Edgar Allan Poe
John Irving
Stephen King

ARTISTS:
Ingres
Leonardo da Vinci

coat color, pattern, hair length and texture, length of tail and number of toes to track the cat's population spread throughout America. The polydactyl trait that gives cats more than their normal five toes per foot is seen most frequently in New England and northward through Newfoundland. There is no evidence that polydactyly occurred naturally in Europe before that time, so it is assumed that the mutation sprang up in the Boston area during the time of its early settlement.

Today, the cat seems to have secured a positive place in our culture and a comfortable one in our homes. America has developed a love affair with the cat that is unprecedented since its domestication. Running neck and neck in popularity with the dog, cats occupy more than fifty billion homes. Cat owners spend more than $3.5 billion on pet food and $300 million on litter every year.

AILUROPHOBES

People who dislike cats are called ailurophobes. Julius Caesar and Voltaire were ailurophobes. Henry III fainted at the sight of a cat. Napolean so disliked cats that he broke out in a sweat every time he saw one, even the tiniest kitten. It is rumored that Johannes Brahms disliked cats so much that he tried to hit them with bow and arrow. U.S. president Dwight D. Eisenhower ordered cats on his Gettysburg farm to be shot.

Cats have helped humankind exterminate rodents from plague-carrying rats to barnyard mice.

Test Your Cat Knowledge

How much do you already know about cats? Take the following true/false quiz to test your cat I.Q. Find the

answers to the questions by reading the rest of the book, or turn to the end of Chapter 14.

1. The first domestic cats appeared in ancient Egypt. True or false

2. Most calico cats are female. True or false

3. The Manx cat is the only tailless breed. True or false

4. Implanting a microchip in a cat is a safe form of identification. True or false

5. Poinsettias are poisonous to cats. True or false

6. Cats can exist on a vegetarian diet. True or false

7. Ringworm is a fungal infection of the skin. True or false

8. Spaying and neutering a cat will make it fat. True or false

9. Not all cats respond to catnip. True or false

10. Spraying and urinating outside of the litter box are the same thing. True or false

11. Training your cat should be based on positive rewards rather than on punishment. True or false

12. Only purebred cats may enter a cat show. True or false

Today, we have a positive relationship with cats in our homes and lives.

chapter 2

The
Domestic
Shorthair

Alley cat, street cat, stray cat, mixed breed, random breed are all names used to describe the domestic shorthaired cat. Found in all sizes (lean and lithe, short and stocky, large and full-bodied), an endless variety of coat patterns (solid orbicolor, spotted, tabby or calico) and a multitude of colors (black, white, gray, brown or orange), the domestic shorthair is the source from which all pedigreed cats spring. Add to these a range of different eye colors—amber, yellow, hazel, green or blue and the shades in between—and you will find there is no limit to the combinations of physical features that make each domestic shorthair unique.

2

The Domestic
Shorthair

Among the many varieties of coat patterns and color combinations found in the domestic shorthair, four are so striking that they have been given names: the calico, tortoiseshell, tabby and tuxedo.

The Calico

In the Newberry Medal award–winning children's book, *The Cat Who Went to Heaven,* a calico cat named Good Fortune brings luck to her Japanese master and teaches him a lesson about kindness and compassion.

In Japanese culture, the calico cat continues to be a symbol of good luck, and small calico cat figurines are often seen in the Japanese home.

In the real feline world, a calico cat is most often white with patches of orange (called red by cat fanciers) and black. Blue-cream calicos have white hair with patches of gray and tan. In the cat fancy world, a gray cat is called blue. As a general rule, the white area covers about two-thirds of a calico's body.

No one is certain where or when the term "calico," as it is applied to a cat's three-tone coat color, originated. One theory is that the calico pattern reminded people of calico fabric, which originated in Calcutta, India.

Most calicos are female. The gene that changes the black coat color to orange (red) and causes the colorful calico patches on the white coat is a sex-linked gene and occurs most commonly in females because of complex genetic combinations.

CALICO CAT REGISTRY INTERNATIONAL

In 1978, cat lover Judith Lindley founded the Calico Cat Registry International to gather and disseminate information about calico cats. The purpose of her organization is to allow full recognition of the calico and the tortoiseshell and to educate people about the rarities that occur within those coat color patterns.

Anyone who owns a calico or tortoiseshell cat, whether he is a mixed breed or purebred, can register him with the organization. Registry requires at least two photos of the cat showing left and right sides and the face, as well as any unusual markings. Registry of males requires at least three photos and a certified letter from a veterinarian stating the cat is a male, noting his age and color, and describing anything unusual about his appearance. The Calico Cat Registry International has thirty rare male calicos and torties registered with it. To obtain a membership application, see Chapter 14, "Resources," for the address.

13

The rare male calico occurs on the average only once in 3,000 calico kittens. Because of the abnormality in the chromosome makeup of male calicos, they are often sterile.

Calico cats are almost always female.

The Tortoiseshell

Tortoiseshell cats are associated with good fortune in Scotland, Ireland, England and France.

The tortoiseshell cat, or tortie for short, carries the same color genes, red and black, as the calico. But instead of having bold patches of color on his coat, the tortoiseshell has a mottled coat pattern in which the red hair is mixed in with the black as though an artist had flecked the hair lightly with a brush dipped in red paint. If the tortie's hair is gray mixed with tan, he is called a blue tortoiseshell. Torties may carry a white spotting gene, which creates a tortie and white cat.

Over the centuries, tortoiseshell cats also have been considered to be good luck. Legend has it that in Scotland and Ireland, it is a good omen when a stray tortoiseshell cat takes up residence in one's home. It is believed that Japanese fishermen take a tortoiseshell cat to sea with them to protect them from the ghosts of their ancestors. A French proverb says that anyone with a tortoiseshell cat is safe from fevers. In England, the close proximity to a tortoiseshell cat supposedly helped a person develop the power of clairvoyance.

In your home, a tortie will provide you with the same companionship and love that all cats do.

The Tabby

Late-night talk-show host, Jay Leno, has one. So does Stella Stevens. Orson Bean owns two. Singers Mickey Gilley and Joy Lynn White each have one, as do artists Mary Engelbert and Leslie Ann Ivory. Actors Jamie Lee Curtis, Mary Fran and Mimi Rogers all have one, and so does baseball player Brian McRae. What do all of these people have? They all are proud owners of one of the most popular cats in America—the tabby.

Today's tabby carries the wild markings of his early feline ancestors.

Tabby cats exist in four basic coat patterns: the mackerel, or striped, pattern; the classic blotched tabby; the spotted tabby; and the Abyssinian, or ticked, tabby. Tabbies come in any of a host of colors—brown, blue, cinnamon, orange, cream or silver, and in any size or body type. The tabby pattern can exist in both mixed breed and purebred cats. Tabbies also can carry the white spotting gene, which creates a combination of tabby and white.

Today's striped tabby is called the "wild" type and still carries the markings typical of his wild ancestors. The

15

tabby pattern is created by dark stripings on a lighter background color called "agouti." Agouti hairs have a bluish base and darker tip separated by a lighter, yellowish stripe. The agouti gene is what causes a cat to have a tabby pattern. Absence of this gene produces a solid-color cat.

Morris serves as the spokescat for 9-Lives™ cat food, as well as for numerous cat welfare projects.

MORRIS THE CAT

One of the most famous tabby cats in the world is Morris, the feline spokescat for 9-Lives™ cat food. In 1968, the first Morris was "discovered" in the Hinsdale Humane Society shelter outside Chicago. Robust and rather laid back, the macho Morris developed feline finickiness into an artform. In addition to making it big in television commercials, Morris was featured in the movie *Shamus,* starring Burt Reynolds and Dyan Cannon, and was dubbed the "Clark Gable of cats."

After Morris died in 1979 at the age of nineteen, 9-Lives™ found a second Morris that looked just like the original, also in a Chicago animal shelter. The second Morris continued the finicky tradition begun by the first tabby. Morris II even had his own magazine, "The Morris Report," in which he always appeared in a centerfold spread.

Since the beginning of the first Morris' career, the 9-Lives™ cats have made national television appearances with such celebrities as Bob Hope and Lily Tomlin. Morris was the first animal actor to be featured as a guest on *Lifestyles of the Rich and Famous,* and he also appeared on *Entertainment Tonight, Good Morning America,* and *The Oprah Winfrey Show.* Morris also was selected by "Young Miss Magazine" as one of the world's most admired males.

For seventeen years, Morris served as spokescat for Adopt-A-Cat month, which benefited the American Humane Association and 1,000 animal shelters nationwide. After serving as 9-Lives™ spokescat for fifteen years, Morris II retired in 1994. Heinz Pet Products, makers of 9-Lives™, announced the same year that it had found Morris III. In keeping with the tradition, Morris III embarked on a campaign to encourage cat owners to care responsibly for their cats. When not in front of the camera, Morris III lives in Chicago with his friend and handler.

Though he appears formally dressed, Socks, the first family's cat, has the comical, down-to-earth quality that makes the tuxedo cat so charming.

The Tuxedo

Tuxedo cats have a predominance of black hair on their bodies, with white paws and white bibs on their necks. They often have white cheeks with white whiskers that seem to explode from their faces like Fourth of July fireworks, giving them a wide-eyed, humorous expression. The white bib and white "spats" make them appear to be dressed for a formal occasion, hence the name "tuxedo."

Over the years, tuxedo cats have been praised by authors, and their humorous appearance has been the inspiration for many a cartoon and book character. In his book, *Old Possum's Book of Practical Cats*, on which the musical *Cats* was based, T. S. Eliot describes tuxedos as merry and bright with cheerful faces "and pleasant to hear when they caterwaul."

When Looney Tunes character Tweety Bird chirped, "I tought I taw a putty tat," he was referring to his black-and-white cat adversary, the spluttering Sylvester. Created by cartoonist Friz Freleng, tuxedo Sylvester, with his white paws and white cheeks and whiskers, achieved fame and notoriety with his animated antics on the silver screen. Like Sylvester, Felix the Cat, a tuxedo character drawn by Australian cartoonist Pat Sullivan, starred in more than eighty films and even had a song written about him.

The same white spotting gene that causes the white color on a calico creates the tuxedo look on a black cat. The black-and-white markings of the tuxedo are most often found in mixed-breed cats.

FIRST CAT SOCKS

When President Bill Clinton and his family moved into 1600 Pennsylvania Avenue in Washington, D.C., they brought with them the first feline to occupy that residence since Jimmy Carter left office in 1981. Unlike his most recent presidential feline predecessors, which were purebred Siamese, Socks has the down-to-earth quality and comical appearance that is typically tuxedo.

The presence of Socks in The White House spawned a whole industry of Socks-related paraphernalia—t-shirts, bumper stickers, keychains and more. Socks even has his own fan club (see Chapter 14, "Resources").

The inspiration for 25 to 30 pieces of mail a month, Socks receives many questions from children wanting to know what it's like to be a cat living in The White House.

chapter 3

The Shorthaired Breeds

Love and appreciation of purebred cats and the unique qualities of the individual breeds is called cat fancy. A purebred cat is one who is registered with a cat association and whose lineage is traceable. The first cat show was held in London's Crystal Palace in 1871. Among the purebred cats exhibited were Abyssinians, Manxes, Siamese and what are now considered British Shorthairs.

The beginnings of the cat fancy in the United States occurred with the first

show held at Madison Square Garden in 1895. At that time the American Cat Club was formed and became the first national registry of purebred cats. The club disbanded the following year, but in 1904, the American Cat Association formed to register cats and became the first U.S. feline registry to last until the present day.

Today, there are six registries of purebred cats in the United States: the American Association of Cat Enthusiasts, the American Cat Association, the American Cat Fanciers' Association, the Cat Fanciers' Association, the Cat Fanciers' Federation and The International Cat Association (TICA). Of the six, the Cat Fanciers' Association is the largest.

Each registry differs in the breeds that it recognizes. In addition, people involved in the cat fancy are continually developing new breeds by crossing existing breeds or developing spontaneous mutations that appear in cats. In the future, you may find cats not listed here appearing in shows or for sale.

Abyssinian

Abyssinian

Picture a cat who resembles a small cougar with a lean body, slightly large ears, and a beautiful ticked coat. Add a slightly impish expression, and you have the Abyssinian. The ticking effect is caused by hair shafts that are a combination of colors. The lighter color lies closest to the skin, followed by darker bands and a dark tip at the end of the shaft. Abyssinians, or Abys for short, come in several colors—ruddy, sorrel, blue, fawn, cream, lilac and silver.

No one is quite sure of the origin of the Abyssinian, but theories abound. One says that the Aby is a direct descendent of ancient Egyptian sacred cats. Another says that the breed originated in Africa and was brought to England by soldiers during the Abyssinian War in the 1860s. Whatever its origins, the Aby first came to America in the early 1900s.

POPULAR BREEDS

According to the Cat Fanciers' Association, the most popular breeds of shorthaired cats are:

Siamese
Abyssinian
Exotic
Scottish Fold
American Shorthair

Aby breeders and owners attest to the Aby's loving nature, its intelligence and gregarious personality. The Abyssinian may be ideal for families with children or other pets.

American Curl Shorthair

American Curl Shorthair

One of the newer breeds on the block is the American Curl. Distinguished by ears that curl back, the American Curl's ears are the antithesis of those of the Scottish Fold, another shorthaired breed.

In 1981, a breeder found a slender, black female cat on the streets of California. Shulamith, as she was named, had interesting ears that turned back from her face. Half of the litter born to her and a local tomcat also had the curled ears. Selective breeding and record keeping began in 1983 by dedicated fanciers.

Today, curls are still slender in build, with a silky, soft coat. American Curl kittens look like any other cat at birth, but in one to seven days, the ears start to curl back. The American Curl is found with both short-haired and longhaired coats and in a variety of color combinations.

*American
Shorthair*

American Shorthair

To the untrained eye, the American Shorthair may look ordinary or common, but the breed is the culmination of a carefully controlled program dedicated to preserving the beauty and temperament of the domestic shorthair. Ironically, the first shorthaired cat registered in the United States was born in Britain and brought to this country in 1901. After native-born felines were incorporated into the breed, "domestic" was added to the shorthair designation. In 1966 the breed name was changed to "American Shorthair."

American Shorthairs average ten to twelve pounds in weight. They have wide-eyed, sweet expressions; muscular frames; and a dense coat of short, thick hair.

American Shorthairs are found in many hair patterns and colors. The silver, classic tabby pattern is often thought of as the most striking.

American Shorthairs have been crossed with existing breeds to create new breeds such as the Exotic Shorthair, Ocicat and Scottish Fold.

American Wirehair

American Wirehair

The cat who started the American Wirehair line was a red tabby-and-white male named Council Rock Farm Adam of Hi-Fi born to a barn cat in 1966. The American Wirehair is similar in conformation to the American Shorthair, except that it has a kinky, wiry coat. The Wirehair is solidly built and muscular. The coat colors and patterns of the Wirehair come in many varieties—solids, bicolors and tabbies.

Breeders and owners of American Wirehairs attest to their friendliness, sensitivity, companionship and love of people.

Bengal

What do you get when you cross an Asian leopard cat with a domestic shorthair? A cat with the look of the wild without the temperament problems of the wild species.

In 1963, a breeder named Jean Mill successfully mated an Asian leopard—a wild cat about the size of a large domestic shorthair, with dark spots on its body and bold stripes on its head—with a domestic shorthair in an effort to satisfy the pet consumer's desire for an exotic pet without the inherent dangers. Thanks to the continuing work of Mill and other breeders over the years, the Bengal has become a recognized breed.

Bengal

Bengals are about the size of an American Shorthair, with beautifully spotted or marbled coats with high contrast between the pattern and background. The tail has a distinctive black tip. Bengals have long, hard, muscular bodies with massive paws, shoulders and legs. They also have loving, outgoing personalities, and they are highly intelligent, curious and, of course, use the litter box.

Bombay

Another look of the wild was captured by a breeder in the 1960s when she began crossing the Burmese with black domestic shorthairs. The resulting cat had sleek, shiny black hair, a muscular body with rounded head and copper eyes and the exotic look reminiscent of the black panther.

Although exotic looking, Bombays have sweet, gentle dispositions and loving personalities. Their easy-going ways enable them to get along with other pets.

Bombay

British Shorthair

What the American Shorthair is to North America, the British Shorthair is to Great Britain, tracing its roots back 2,000 years when the conquering Romans brought cats with them to the shores of the British Isles. At the first cat show held at London's Crystal Palace in 1871 were many British Shorthairs in a variety of coat colors besides the traditional blue.

*British
Shorthair*

The British Shorthair was bred with Persians and other foreign cats following World War II, and its look changed toward a chunkier body, a plusher coat and a shorter, broader face. The British Shorthair is compact and powerful. Mature "Brits," as they are called, weigh anywhere from twelve to seventeen pounds. Owners of Brits claim that they are quiet and intelligent and that their cuddly nature makes them good pets for children.

Burmese

If you want an active, entertaining cat to share your home, the Burmese may be for you. Lineage of this sable-colored breed can be traced to a cat named Wong Mau who first arrived in the United States with a sailor from Rangoon in 1930.

The Burmese is of medium size and good muscular development and has sweet, expressive eyes. Acceptable coat colors include platinum and champagne, as well as sable.

Burmese

California Spangled Cat

Unlikely as it may seem, if you combine genetic characteristics of the Abyssinian, Angora, Manx, Siamese and British and American Shorthairs, the resulting cat looks nothing like any one of them. Add to the mix a small feral cat from Egypt and a tropical house cat from Southeast Asia, and the result is a spotted feline with the wild look of the jungle, yet fully capable of living healthily and happily in your home.

California Spangled kitten

The California Spangled Cat was literally "designed" in the 1970s by Paul Casey, whose objective was to give people a house pet with the same beautifully spotted coat as a leopard. The California Spangled Cat made a flurry of a furry debut in the Nieman-Marcus Christmas catalog in 1986. Despite the high price tag, its creator had orders for more than three hundred fifty cats. Although applicants for the new breed were carefully screened, the event was not without its controversy among animal lovers.

The California Spangled Cat is large, well-muscled, athletic and graceful and comes in a variety of coat colors. Its lack of wild ancestry makes it a cat without any problems in temperament.

Chartreux

Legend says that the Chartreux, the blue cat of France, originated when a monk of Le Grande Chartreux Order, the same monks world famous for their Liqueur des Pères Chartreux, brought one to the French Alps in the 17th century to be used as a mouser in the monastery. The Chartreux had been a French staple for a very long time before being introduced to the U.S. cat fancy in 1970.

Chartreux

Often confused with the British Shorthair, Russian Blue or Korat, the Chartreux has a robust, well-muscled body and can weigh up to fourteen pounds. Its coat is medium long, with a dense, woolly undercoat. It comes in only one color—blue. The Chartreux has a rounded head with a mouth that seems to smile and bright, rounded eyes that give it an endearing, friendly appearance. The Chartreux has a gentle, fun-loving nature and is an active companion.

Welcome to
the World of
Shorthaired
Cats

Colorpoint Shorthair

The Colorpoint Shorthair is a hybrid created in the 1940s by crossing the Siamese with the Abyssinian and red domestic shorthair. Although resembling the Siamese in its medium-sized, slender body with a tapered head and large pointed ears, the Colorpoint comes in a variety of colors besides the traditional seal, blue, chocolate and lilac points. Colorpoint varieties include Creampoint, striped Lynxpoint, multicolored Tortiepoint and a Himalayan pattern.

*Colorpoint
Shorthair*

The Colorpoint, like its Siamese cousin, is outgoing, talkative and very intelligent.

Cornish Rex

Cornish Rex

Named after the Rex rabbit, the Cornish Rex has a wavy coat over its entire body and short, curly whiskers that are the result of a spontaneous mutation. Discovered in Cornwall, England, in 1950, the ancestor of the present-day Cornish line was a curly, cream-colored male kitten named Kallibunker born to a domestic farm cat. Although it may appear fragile, the Cornish Rex is a combination of grace and strength.

The coat is made up of rows of dense, tight curls that are soft to the touch. The curly coat comes in a variety of colors and coat patterns.

Playful and people oriented, the Cornish Rex has a devilish sense of humor to delight the most discriminating pet owner.

Devon Rex

Although the Devon Rex shares a curly coat and body type with the Cornish Rex, the curly-haired trait was caused by different mutations in each cat. Like its cousin, the Devon Rex was discovered in England, but in Devonshire, not Cornwall, ten years after the discovery of the curly kitten that started the Cornish Rex breed.

Devon Rex

Like the Cornish Rex, the Devon is recognized in almost every color and coat pattern, although its coat is less plush and swirls in all directions rather than in a uniform, wavy pattern. It has a medium frame and the distinctive Rex head with large, prominant ears.

Egyptian Mau

You've read about the Bengal and the California Spotted Cat, two wild-looking pedigrees that were

created by humans through carefully planned breeding programs. Now meet the Egyptian Mau, a lovely,
spotted cat whose coat is the work of Mother Nature
herself. No human intervention was required to create
the wild look of this feline.

Egyptian Mau

*Exotic
Shorthair*

The Egyptian Mau is the oldest of the spotted
variety of felines, tracing its origins back to ancient
Egypt. The first Mau was brought to the States
in 1956 by Princess Natalie
Troubetskoye, a Russian princess
living in exile.

Maus tend to bond with one or
two family members and are
somewhat shy with strangers.
Extremely intelligent cats, they
tend to be more quiet around the
house. Maus come in a variety
of acceptable colors, including
bronze, silver, smoke and pewter.

Exotic Shorthair

If you want a cat that looks like
a Persian but does not require
so much grooming, the Exotic
Shorthair (called simply Exotic by CFA), is the cat for
you. With hair that is short but plush; the characteristic

Persian face, with the pushed-in nose and bright, wide eyes; and a short, heavy, compact body (called "cobby"), the Exotic is a beautiful and endearing breed.

Exotics come in more than forty-five colors, including solid and bicolors, as well as particolors. Exotics even come in a pointed color, which resembles a shorthaired Himalayan. They are affectionate and playful.

Havana Brown

Ironically, the Havana Brown did not originate in Havana or anywhere else in Cuba for that matter. No one is entirely sure where the name Havana Brown originated, but brown cats appeared in cat shows in Britain for almost a hundred years. The first Havanas arrived in the U.S. in the 1950s and developed into a cat that no longer resembles the Siamese-type cat known in England. Havana Browns are of medium size, with a rich, mahogany-brown coat and green eyes.

Havana Brown

Havanas are even-tempered, affectionate and social cats. They are very people oriented and love human companionship.

31

Japanese Bobtail

The Japanese Bobtail is one of two tailless shorthaired breeds. Originally imported to the U.S. in 1968, the Bobtail is known to have inhabited Japan since the sixth century. Although Bobtails come in all colors, the traditional three-color, called Mi-Ke, meaning "three-fur" in Japanese, is prized among breeders because of its history.

*Japanese
Bobtail*

The Japanese Bobtail is an active breed, sleek and slender, with clean lines and bone structure. The bobbed tail resembles that of a rabbit and is usually about three inches long, with one or more curves or kinks. No two tails are alike.

Korat

Korat

If you want to have a cat that may bring you good luck as well as happiness, the Korat may be the cat for you. Korats originated in Siam, now Thailand, as early as the 14th century. Depicted in a manuscript dating from A.D. 1350 called *Cat-Book Poems,* the Korat is one of nineteen cats thought to bring their owners good fortune.

The Korat is a silver-blue color with silver tipping and no shading or markings. It is medium-sized, with green or amber eyes. Breeders say that Korats bond closely with their owners and prefer the feline companionship of other Korats to cats of other breeds.

Manx

Manx

A famous legend says that the Manx lost its tail when Noah was ushering pairs of animals into the ark. Because the cat was securing a mouse in preparation for the long journey, he waited until the last minute to come aboard, squeezing in as Noah slammed the door behind him, accidentally cutting off his tail.

The truth is that the Manx, the other tailless shorthaired breed, is one of the oldest breeds of cats, although no records exist of its exact origin. It is known to have inhabited the Isle of Man in the Irish Sea for many centuries. Because no cats were indigenous to the Isle of Man, it is assumed that they were brought there by

> **FAMOUS OWNERS OF PUREBREEDS**
>
> **Abyssinians:** Robert Goulet, Poly Bergen
>
> **Oriental Shorthair:** Sally Jesse Raphael
>
> **Siamese:** Amy Carter, daughter of former President Jimmy Carter; Susan Ford, daughter of former President Gerald Ford

humans. The taillessness is thought to be a result of a spontaneous mutation.

Taillessness in the Manx is caused by a dominant gene rather than a recessive one, as in the Bobtail. Because the Manx gene can produce spinal deformities and colon defects, kittens who inherit the gene from both parents often don't survive.

The Manx tail comes in a variety of lengths and is described as a rumpy (no tail), rumpy-riser (a short knobby tail), stumpy (a short or kinked tail) or longy (a virtually normal-looking tail).

The Manx is a solidly muscled cat with rounded body, rounded head with prominent cheeks and large, wide eyes. The coat comes in all varieties of colors and patterns. Manx cats are loving and get along with other pets and family members.

Ocicat

Ocicat

How would you like to share your home with a cat who has the coat of a spotted ocelot and a pussycat personality? The ocicat is another hybrid that is the result of crossbreeding Abyssinians, Siamese and the American Shorthair. No wild cats were involved in creating the Ocicat breed.

Ocicats can reach a weight of up to fifteen pounds. Their bodies are firm and muscular. Ocicats come in twelve colors, including chocolate, tawny and cinnamon. They are fun loving and affectionate.

Oriental Shorthair

In the 1950s and 60s, breeders wanted a cat that resembled a Siamese but in additional colors. Cross-breeding Abyssinians, Siamese and American Shorthairs, they developed the Oriental Shorthair, a cat with the personality and body type of a Siamese—slender body, wedge-shaped head, large ears—but with a mix of color combinations to please just about any cat fancier. Oriental Shorthairs come in nine base colors and six color combinations. The colors can appear in a variety of patterns—solid, shaded, smoke or tabby. They can have the agouti ticking of an Aby or the spots of an ocicat. In addition, they come in the pointed patterns of the Siamese.

*Oriental
Shorthair*

As colorful as the Oriental Shorthair is in coat, it has a personality to match. People-oriented Oriental Shorthairs like to share your activities and are extremely talkative.

Russian Blue

The first Russian Blues competed in England in the early part of this century. Called Foreign Blues, they competed along with every other type of blue cat in the same category. Serious breeding of Russian Blues did

Russian Blue

not begin in the United States until the late 1940s.

Russian Blues have fine bones and firm muscles. The body type is the slender variety of the category known as "foreign," which includes cats such as the Siamese. It comes in only one color, blue, for which it is named. Russian Blues have vivid green eyes.

Russian Blues are more shy with strangers than other breeds of cats. Although they are friendly and comfortable with members of their human family, they are among the more sensitive of breeds.

Scottish Fold

Scottish Folds, those adorable, huggable cats with the folded down ears, trace their ancestry to a white barn

Scottish Fold

cat named Susie, discovered in Scotland in 1961. The ears of a Fold can vary from slightly forward-tilting to tightly folded.

Folds have dense, plush hair, wide eyes and cobby bodies. Perpetually playful, they are also devoted companions and love to lie on owners' laps.

Selkirk Rex

One of the newest Rex breeds to be recognized by cat fancier associations is the Selkirk Rex. Created by crossbreeding a Persian with a curly-haired kitten found at a shelter, the breed was further developed by outcrossing with the American and British Shorthairs in the late 1980s.

Selkirk Rex

The distinctive feature of the Selkirk Rex is the curly hair that is plush and full. Unlike its cousins, the Devon and Cornish Rex, the Selkirk's coat comes in both shorthaired and longhaired versions.

Siamese

One of the oldest and most well known of the pure-bred cats is the Siamese. It is also one of the most popular among breeders and cat lovers everywhere. As distinctive sounding as it is distinctive looking, the Siamese was named after its place of origin, Siam, now Thailand. Treasured by the royalty of Siam, the cat was often presented as a gift to people around the world.

Siamese cats were first exhibited at cat shows in England in 1871 and came to the United States in the early 1900s. An imported Siamese is reported to have cost a minimum of $1,000—a hefty price for a pet at the turn of the century.

The Siamese is now ranked as the most popular short-haired breed by the Cat Fanciers' Association. Because of its popularity, the Siamese has been a source for crossbreeding to create new breeds such as the Colorpoint Shorthair, Oriental Shorthair and Ocicat.

Siamese

The look of the Siamese has gone through some changes since its introduction into the cat fancy.

Singapura

The earlier version of the breed had a somewhat heavier body and a more rounded head. The current version of the Siamese has the long, slender foreign body type with a wedge-shaped head. Proponents of both types claim that theirs most resembles the original Siamese imported from Siam.

The Siamese's unique appearance, striking "conversational" ability and outgoing personality make it a star among purebreds.

Singapura

The Singapura is a natural breed native to Southeast Asia. Imported to the U.S. in 1975 by a breeder who reportedly found the original cats on the streets of Singapore the previous year, the dainty Singapura comes in one color only—a dark brown ticking on a warm ivory ground color.

Singapuras are small to medium in size, with a slightly stocky, muscular body. Their eyes are brilliant green or haze yellow, and their wide-eyed expressions give them a playful look. People who breed or own Singapuras claim they are people oriented and actively interested in all of their owners' activities.

Snowshoe

The Snowshoe is considered a mitted breed—one that has white mittens on its feet—and is the only mitted breed boasting a short coat of hair instead of a long one. The Snowshoe is the result of developing characteristics that resulted from the breeding of two Siamese in the 1960s.

"THE CAT WHO" MYSTERIES

Author and Siamese cat lover Lilian Jackson Braun incorporates two Siamese cat characters into her *The Cat Who . . .* mystery series. Feline sleuths YumYum and Koko have helped the main character, Jim Quilleran, solve more than seventeen mysteries with such titles as *The Cat Who Blew the Whistle, The Cat Who Moved a Mountain* and *The Cat Who Came to Breakfast.*

Braun lives in North Carolina with her husband and two real-life Siamese cats, Koko III and Pitti Sing.

Snowshoe

Snowshoes are medium in size. They are friendly cats and get along well with other pets in the household.

Sphynx

For the cat lover who hates grooming, the Sphynx offers a carefree alternative. Although it appears to be completely bald, the Sphynx is actually covered with a fine, soft down, but needless to say, requires no combing and brushing.

The Sphynx is the result of spontaneous mutations and was developed as a distinct breed. Originally named the New Mexican Hairless, its name was changed to the more regal-sounding Sphynx.

In appearance, the Sphynx body is similar to those of the Cornish and Devon Rex breeds. It has very large ears, wide eyes and almost no whiskers. The Sphynx may

Sphynx

have a variety of patterns and colors that appear as coloration of the skin rather than coat.

Tonkinese

Tonkinese

The Tonkinese originated in the 1960s as a result of crossing a Siamese with a Burmese. The Tonkinese, or "Tonk," has a body type that is in between the slender body of the Siamese and the cobby body of the Burmese. Tonks are medium in size, with almond-shaped, aqua eyes. Their coats are a "mink" pattern of lighter body color with correspondingly distinct, darker points. Different registries accept different colors, including blue mink, champagne mink, honey mink, natural mink and platinum mink.

chapter 4

Your
Individual
Cat

You and your cat will spend many years together, so finding the right cat for your personality, home environment and lifestyle will help contribute to a lasting friendship with your feline roommate.

Cats require care and attention, but some cats may require more than others. Cats with thick coats or undercoats will require more grooming attention than those with shorter, sleeker hair. Allowing your cat outside may eliminate some of the litter box chores for you, but will increase the grooming and bathing activities and most certainly will require added attention in the flea-fighting department.

The size of your living area—small apartment or large, multiroom house—may determine the kind of cat you adopt. Typically, more active breeds such as the Abyssinian, Colorpoint Shorthair, Siamese or Japanese Bobtail will want plenty of space to jump and climb. Larger breeds such as the American Shorthair, Bengal or British Shorthair or larger, domestic shorthairs may need a bit more breathing room than an efficiency apartment provides.

Families with children will be satisfied with a friendly, patient Manx.

If you have other pets, you may want to consider a cat who gets along with other animals such as the Bombay, Manx or Snowshoe. If you have an active lifestyle and want a cat whose personality matches your outgoing ways or simply one who is very people oriented, try an American Wirehair, Cornish Rex or Korat. If you have children, you may want to adopt a domestic shorthair or breeds such as the British Shorthair, Exotic or Manx. Also, families with small children should stay away from cats who typically bond with one or two family members such as the Siamese or Egyptian Mau.

Finding the Right Cat

Once you have decided what kind of cat to adopt, you must find a place to obtain one. If you would like to share your home with a purebred cat, purchasing one from a reputable breeder will help ensure her good health and pleasing personality. A good breeder will help you choose the right cat and will be able to provide you with a pet-quality purebred at a lower cost than a show-quality one if you are not interested in showing.

To find a reputable breeder in your area, ask your veterinarian for recommendations, attend a local cat show and talk to breeders who are exhibiting, or check the breeder directories in the national cat magazines.

Be sure to ask questions when you talk to a breeder. Ask for more detailed information about the breed and its basic personality. Describe your living situation and ask whether the breed is a good match. If the breeder is local, ask to visit the cattery. Find out whether the cats are part of the household (and therefore more socialized) or are kept in a separate area.

A cat from a shelter can be a wonderful, loving pet.

Shelter Cats

If you want a domestic shorthaired cat with no pedigree, you can find one in just about any size or color at a local shelter. If the shelter is a good one, cats in their care will be well-fed and receive veterinary medical care if necessary. Some shelters are called no-kill because the animals stay at the shelter until adopted. Unfortunately, space is often limited in no-kill facilities, so shelters that take in the excess animals are forced to euthanize them if they are not adopted in a predetermined number of days.

When you visit a shelter, talk to the staff about the cats who interest you. Find out as much as possible about them. Some shelters keep information on file about where each cat came from and why the cat was brought to the shelter. Not all cats are turned over to shelters for reasons having anything to do with the cat. Many are surrendered for the most fatuous of reasons. "We're moving," "I'm having a baby," "We're getting divorced" are excuses people use when their pet becomes inconvenient and they wish to discard her. The unfortunate animals who have given them companionship and love are now abandoned through no fault of their own.

Kittens are certainly charming, but an older cat should not be considered an undesirable adoption candidate.

Most people who want to adopt a cat choose a kitten. While the antics of a playful kitten are a joy to behold, an older cat should not be looked upon as an undesirable adoption candidate. In many cases, these cats are already spayed or neutered, tested for infectious disease and trained to live in a human environment.

Breeders also may have older purebred cats available who were once part of the show circuit but have slowed down a bit and no longer enjoy competition or are no longer a part of a breeding program. Although most breeders consider their cats to be loving pets and members of their households, occasionally they put older show cats up for adoption to loving owners if they decide to reduce the number of cats they have in their catteries.

Naming Your Cat

Once you have selected a cat, you must name her. Even if you adopt an older cat who already has a name, you can give her another name to which the cat will learn to respond in no more time than it took for her to learn her first name. In fact, as your cat's personality begins to reveal itself, you may find yourself giving your cat multiple nicknames, all of which will become part of your cat's repertoire of understanding.

"The Naming of Cats is a difficult matter," said T. S. Eliot in *Old Possum's Book of Practical Cats.* Naming a cat after a person, whether famous or simply a friend, is one way to go about the task. If a particular subject or part of history interests you, give your cat a name from that era. Roosevelt, Lincoln or Churchill are names of statesmen that might be appropriate for the more dignified feline. You might like to name your cat after a television, movie or novel character.

A safe collar is a good method of identification for your cat.

If you are a *Star Trek* fan, for example, Spock, Data or Worf might be suitable names. Two siblings might be appropriately called Crocket and Tubbs. Charlie Chan and Hercule Poirot are names of two famous sleuths for the more curious and investigative cat.

If your cat is a breed that bears the name of a particular country, such as an Egyptian Mau, Burmese, British Shorthair, Russian Blue or Siamese, research famous figures or places from the country's history and find one that is suitable for your cat. Bastet for a Mau or Anastasia for a Russian Blue are two examples.

Some people choose to name their cats based on their appearances. Ghost, Crystal or Cotton are names for white cats; Midnight, Ebony or Ink for black cats. Add some variety to common names by finding the word in another language. Bianca is Italian for white, for example. Tiger is a common name for— what else?—the tiger-striped tabby. Cats with white feet are often called Mittens or Socks. An active cat with extra toes on her feet might be named Boxer. A cat with a black spot around her eye could be called Pirate.

Names can combine attributes of the cat's personality and interests of your own. If you are a railroad buff, for example, Caboose might be an enjoyable name, especially if your cat always follows you around. A cat owner into the sewing arts might want to name a fun-loving cat Stitch or a delicate one Crochet. A sports fan might want to name his or her cat after a favorite team—Raider or Mariner depending on whether the cat likes to swipe food from your plate or prefers a good dish of fish.

In choosing a name for your cat, you are limited only by your imagination. Whatever you choose, make the name one of dignity and compassion and one that does not poke fun at your cat or her mannerisms. And make sure the name is not one that will embarrass you in your veterinarian's office when a technician calls your cat into her appointment.

> ## BAKER AND TAYLOR— ADVERTISING CATS
>
> Cats are often featured in advertisements, even for products that have nothing to do with felines. Two widely photographed Scottish Folds have become the trademark for Baker Taylor Books, a company that distributes books and materials.
>
> Baker was adopted in 1983 by a librarian in Minden, Nevada, to work in a rodent-control capacity. The librarian named the cat Baker in honor of the company from which the library purchased materials. The local Baker Taylor Books sales representative was so pleased that he offered to obtain another Fold for them if they named it Taylor.
>
> Baker and Taylor were signed for a lifetime advertising contract with Baker Taylor Books. Baker died in 1995, but the two Scottish Folds continue to appear in ads for the company line.

Identifying Your Cat

Once you have named your cat, it is important to provide her with some form of identification in the event that she becomes lost. Even an indoors-only cat can slip out the door at a moment's notice. Some form of identification on your cat will help her to be returned to you and decrease the chances that she will end up unclaimed in a shelter or be turned over to a medical laboratory.

When you have your cat vaccinated for rabies, your veterinarian will provide her with a tag that can be attached to a collar. Unfortunately, tags can become caught on things, and depending on the type of collar, can choke your cat. Instead of a leather collar, you can make a safe collar by sewing or tying a one-fourth- to one-half-inch piece of elastic with your name and phone number printed in indelible ink or embroidered onto it. If your cat gets caught on a shrub or piece of hedge, the collar will slip off.

Modern technology is providing safe, permanent alternative identification methods to the typical collar and tag. One method is a microchip that can be implanted quickly and safely into your cat by a veterinarian. The microchip is programmed with a unique code that can be identified with a handheld scanner in use in shelters and veterinary offices. The code is then fed into a national database that identifies your pet and you as her owner.

A second method is to have identification tattooed onto your cat. The tattoo is usually placed on the cat's inner thigh. The process takes only a few seconds and is relatively painless. If your cat is a purebred show cat, check with her breed registry to determine whether there are any regulations governing the placement of tattoos.

If you would like to use either of these methods to identify your cat, discuss it with your veterinarian, who will be able to recommend a legitimate registering organization.

If Your Cat Is Lost

If your cat does accidentally become lost, her method of identification will be one step in making sure she is returned home safely. To increase your chances of finding your cat, however, it is wise to post notices in local shelters and veterinarians offices.

Color-copy technology has improved so that you will be able to make your own "wanted" posters bearing a description and color photo of your cat for unmistakable identification.

If Something Happens to You

As unpleasant as it is to think about, accidents do happen. Should you be incapacitated for any length of time, make sure that someone knows you have a cat and is willing to look after her. To help in the task and make sure your cat gets the care she is accustomed to, keep a file on your cat that includes the dates of her vaccinations, her medical history and what she eats. Keep this file where those who need to will be able to find it.

Living

with Your

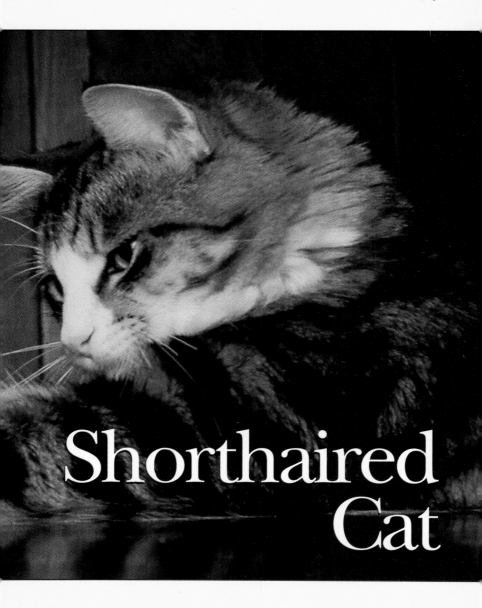

part two

Shorthaired Cat

chapter 5

Your Cat and

Your

Home

The key to a successful relationship with your feline roommate is the old scout motto, "Be prepared." Taking your cat's needs into consideration and planning accordingly will help you create an environment that is safe and fun for your cat and easy to maintain for you.

The "Box"

Some of the most important decisions you will make as a cat owner concern your cat's litter box. What kind of box, what kind of filler, where to place the box and keeping it clean are issues that will determine your cat's attitude about using it. Mistakes in this area or an unwillingness to experiment could have unfortunate results if your cat decides to use another item in your home for his elimination needs.

Most cats, even young kittens, will begin to use cat litter as soon as they are placed in it or shown where the box is. Simply showing your cat the litter box will, in most cases, be enough to get your cat started in his daily routine. Today, however, there are many options for cat boxes and types of filler. A knowledge of what is on the market may help you choose items that not only satisfy your cat but you as well.

Most cats will use the litter box naturally after being shown its location, but some may require more patience to train.

Cat owners need not settle for a litter box that looks like a dishpan. In addition to litter boxes that have curved sides to trap scattered litter when kitty covers his waste, there are covered litter boxes that offer more protection to surrounding walls from cats that stand up to urinate. Some covered boxes have clear plastic hoods or skylights for the more claustrophobic cats who do not like the feeling of being closed in. In addition, twenty-first–century technology has given cat owners the cat box ecosystem, which not only collects and traps kitty's wastes but recycles them as well.

Clay litter has been around for several decades, but even clay comes in scented or unscented varieties. Clay litter is less expensive, but it produces more dust than other types of litter. Among the clay varieties, some are more dust-free than others. Clay litter must be completely dumped periodically to keep it clean.

During the 1990s, manufacturers introduced the sand-based, clumping litter, which produces a patty-like ball of wet sand when kitty urinates in it. The patty is easily lifted out, leaving only clean, dry litter in the box. Sand litter produces a more clean-smelling litter box and, although its initial price is higher than clay litter, is cheaper to use because it does not need to be dumped, simply refreshed as the amount in the box decreases.

Today, more and more ecologically friendly litter products made of wood chips, corn husks, grain or paper are appearing on the market. Some of these litters are completely dust-free and can be flushed down the toilet. When choosing a litter, find one that is acceptable to you, your cat and your pocketbook.

Placement of the litter box will depend on what kind of home you have, but the location should be easily accessible to your cat. The basement may be out of sight for you, but if the floor is always damp, your cat may not want to walk across it to get to the box. Seldom-used bathrooms, shower stalls, laundry or mud rooms are excellent locations for your cat's litter box.

"KITTY LITTER"

More than sixty-four million cats reside in homes across the United States. Many of them live partially or completely indoors. The one event in the history of man's relationship with the domestic feline that is credited with the creation of the indoor cat is the development of cat litter.

First manufactured by Ed Lowe in 1947 from clay garage oil absorbent, cat litter was intended to help cat owners whose cats were unable to bury their waste in winter's frozen soil. Kitty Litter is the name Lowe gave his new product.

Like the word "Xerox," which has become synonymous with photocopy, and the word "Kleenex," which often is used to denote a facial tissue, "Kitty Litter" has become the phrase commonly used by cat owners to describe any of the commercially available cat box fillers.

Since its development, cat litter has become one of the most important products available for cats and their owners. Still marketed today under the same name, Kitty Litter was the feline equivalent of indoor plumbing.

Litter box manufacturers have recently introduced furniture that is equipped with a litter box inside and a door that gives your cat easy access to it. Designed to look like a small chest of drawers or wash stand, these furniture litter boxes fit with most decors and are especially convenient for people living in small apartments. You can find one of these litter boxes by shopping at a local pet store or browsing the classified sections of the national cat magazines (see Chapter 14, "Resources").

Once you have chosen a litter box, filler and location, you will want to make sure that it is kept clean. Nothing discourages a cat from using his box like dirty litter, so remove wastes daily and completely clean the box as necessary. If you are not buying scented litter, add baking soda to the litter to remove odors.

If your cat develops a litter box problem in spite of your good efforts, see Chapter 10, "Your Cat's Behavior," for ways to correct the problem.

Scratch 'n' Sniff

One of your cat's favorite pastimes will be scratching his claws. Animal behaviorists believe that cats have a territorial nature and that scratching is a way for a cat to leave his scent on objects and claim them as his own. But scratching has a more practical purpose. Cats shed their claws regularly, and scratching helps them remove the old sheath that is being pushed out by the new claw.

Whatever the reason, having something for your cat to scratch will make him happy and protect your furniture. Scratch posts come in all sizes and shapes, from the subtle to the, well, large and overpowering. What kind of post you select will depend on the space you have available and how much of it you are willing to allot to it.

Scratch posts are generally made from pieces of wood covered with carpet or sisal, although some combine bare, specially treated tree branches with carpet- or sisal-covered sections. They can be small and have a rope at one end to attach to a door knob. Others are free-standing and can be very complex in construction, with multilevels for your cat to climb. Scratch posts can cost from less than $10 to more than $1,000 for the really elaborate ones. If you are handy with hammer and saw, you can make your own.

If you have upholstered furniture, there are ways to protect it from cats who may eyeball it as a substitute for a scratch post. Making your furniture unappealing in feline terms will deter your cat from sinking his claws into it. Wicker and rattan are an open invitation for your cat's clawing instincts. Buying furniture with textured fabrics is tantamount to putting a flashing neon "Claw me!" sign on your furniture. Fabrics that are more tightly woven or have a smooth surface such as velour are a feline's least favorite material.

If you want an iron-clad method of keeping your cat from clawing your upholstered furniture, cover it with a plastic covering or purchase molded Lucite pieces that fit over sofa ends, the place where cats typically claw. Better yet, buy wooden furniture such as futons to dissuade your cat entirely.

The Pros and Cons of Declawing

Most cats can be trained to use a scratch post instead of furniture, but some cat owners who cannot or prefer not to train their cats to scratch a post elect to declaw their cats in order to fully protect their furniture and property. Declawing is a process whereby the end bone of the digit holding the claw on each toe, generally on the front two paws, is surgically removed. The surgery is performed under anesthesia, and recovery takes from three days to two weeks. Following surgery, the cats paws are bandaged, and several days of hospitalization are required.

People who declaw their cats point to the fact that most veterinarians perform the surgery routinely and that it is generally effective. In addition, those who favor the surgery say it is preferable to declaw a cat than to give him up to a new owner.

Those who object to declawing argue that during the declawing process, all of the germinal tissue must be removed or the claw will grow back. Because of the location of the surgery, movement of the cat when he walks or flexes his toes may cause the incisions to reopen and bleed. Some opponents of declawing feel that the surgery is painful and causes long-term emotional harm to the cat.

Loosely woven, rough material is an invitation for your cat to scratch.

To date, there are no scientific findings to support that declawing a cat causes any long-term emotional or physical problems. If you feel that surgery is too extreme a method of solving a scratching problem, there are alternatives. Invented by a Louisiana veterinarian named Dr. Toby Wexler, Soft Paws (a registered trademark of Soft Paws, Inc.) are soft, vinyl nail clips that are easily applied to your cat's nails. The nail caps cushion the effects of your cat when he scratches, while allowing him to stretch and retract his claws. Available through veterinarians, Soft Paws last about four to six weeks. They even come in colors.

Declawing will impair your cat's ability to climb and defend himself, so if you do decide to declaw your cat, be sure to keep him indoors.

Nap Time

Your cat may spend up to sixteen hours a day sleeping. That amount of time will increase as your cat ages. Most cats want to sleep with their owners, but providing additional sleeping spots will help you keep kitty comfy, as well as control the amount of hair that sticks to your furniture.

Cats love to curl up and sleep in cozy places.

Cats love to sleep in tight places. Providing your cat with adequate sleeping facilities can be as simple as giving him a cardboard box or wicker basket to curl up in. If you want to provide your cat with something more elaborate, manufacturers of cat products have created a wealth of interesting beds to satisfy your cat's cravings. Faux fur kitty cups—round beds with stuffed fabric sides—hug your cat when he's curled up inside. Beds modeled after pup tents for camping, or those that resemble a large running shoe in which your cat can snuggle inside, add a touch of whimsy to your home.

Place your cat's bed anywhere that is comfortable for your cat and convenient for you. Place it on a piece of your furniture to help keep hair deposits to a minimum. Cat beds can be purchased for as little as $10.

Pet Cleanup

Cleaning up after your cat should be relatively easy and not take an inordinate amount of time. Cleaning the litter box takes only a few minutes a day. Depending on the type of litter you choose, you may find pieces scattered around the litter box when your cat exits. To pick up occasional litter from the floor, keep a small vacuum or dustpan and brush handy. Placing a grass doormat in front of the cat box will help remove excess litter from your cat's feet as he exits.

Removing hair from furniture can be accomplished easily and quickly by going over the area with rubber gloves or a washable sticky roller available in discount department stores. Prevent hair buildup by placing your cat's bed, a towel or specially designed cat mat on his favorite sleeping spot.

Tile and hardwood flooring are easier to keep clean but show cat hair more. Carpeting keeps the cat hair down but presents more cleaning challenges. If your cat has an accident on the carpet, remove it quickly and blot up the excess liquid. Use a mild detergent or all-liquid cleaner designed to remove odors as well as clean. Washable bed clothes and fabrics, washable paint and wallpaper will aid in your pet cleanup efforts.

The Great Debate: Indoors or Out?

One of the issues that divides cat owners is whether to keep a cat inside or allow him free access to the outdoors. It is one of the few topics that, when it comes up, usually results in a heated discussion with participants passionately expressing both sides of the issue.

In the past, when the outdoors presented a much calmer, safer environment, it was customary to allow cats to go outside at will. In fact, forty or fifty years ago, it was unusual for cats to be allowed inside the home.

Because of the development of products like Kitty Litter, changes in society making it more dangerous for cats to be outside and the growing numbers of people who live in apartments or condominiums, more and more cats are spending their lives in the great indoors.

People who allow their cats free access to the outdoors feel that a cat should be allowed to enjoy being in the fresh air and the sunshine; to stalk and hunt prey, which is his nature; and to climb trees and explore the natural environment. They believe that the quality of the cat's life is improved by being allowed outside no matter the risk.

Those who keep their cats indoors exclusively, or allow them outside only in an enclosure or on a leash, argue that a free-roaming cat faces danger from traffic, pet thieves, poisonings and mutilations, other free-roaming pets and wild or rabid animals. In addition, outdoor cats are more likely to contract contagious diseases such as feline leukemia, feline infectious peritonitis, feline immunodeficiency virus, and zoonotic diseases—those transmitted from animal to human—such as rabies and toxoplasmosis. One of the more sobering zoonotic diseases that has been detected in free-roaming felines in recent years is bubonic plague. At the very least, outdoor cats fall victim to parasites such as fleas, mites and worms and ultimately bring them back into the house.

An outdoor cat enjoys the air and sunshine but is also more susceptible to diseases and accidents.

As your cat's caregiver, you must decide for yourself whether to keep your cat indoors exclusively or allow him to go outside at will. Recent surveys have shown that more than two-thirds of America's cat owners keep their cats entirely indoors or out only under supervision. Refer to Chapter 9,

"Your Cat's Mental Health," for ways to make the indoors adventuresome and fun.

Indoor Gardens

Cats love to chew on greens, and yours may seek out your houseplants to satisfy his craving. To keep your cat from chewing on your plants, obtain varieties that are unappealing, such as cacti or succulents, or hang your plants from the ceiling to keep them out of your cat's reach. Putting pine cones or stones around the base of your potted plants will keep kitty from digging in the dirt.

If you would like to provide your cat with fresh, edible greens, plant a pot of grass seed for him to eat, or purchase at a pet store prepotted seeds specially packaged for kitty's discriminating tastes.

Plant a pot of grass seed for kitty to chew on.

Poisonous Plants

Many plants are poisonous to cats, including daffodil, English ivy, hydrangea and marijuana, to name just a few. Ingesting them can cause symptoms from labored breathing and vomiting to convulsions and death. It is best not to bring poisonous varieties into your home, regardless of where you put them. If they are a food substance, such as potatoes, keep them out of reach of your cat. The pits of peaches, apricots and cherries, as well as apple seeds, are also toxic to cats. Be sure to dispose of them properly.

Safety First

Cats are naturally curious animals. Your cat's desire to investigate and explore could get him into trouble if you have not taken some safety precautions around the house. Prevention is the best cure, so modify your cat's environment to keep him from coming to harm.

Cats have a preference for small, out-of-the-way places. Cupboards, recliners, clothes dryers and refrigerators beckon a cat who wants a cozy spot in which to hide. Always keeping cupboard and appliance doors closed will prevent kitty from getting into these areas and becoming trapped.

Ironing boards and irons are easily tipped when a cat jumps on them. To prevent your cat from being accidentally hit by a falling iron or board, put them away when not in use.

Mr. Yuk stickers may keep a child from getting into a dangerous substance, but no sticker

Cats can be wonderful friends to children who are gentle and careful with them.

in the world will keep your cat safe from chemical hazards in his environment. Residue from abrasive cleanser or household cleaners left in the sink or tub will adhere to your cat's paws if he walks through them. When your cat washes, ingestion of the cleaning substance could poison him. When cleaning a room, close it off until the surfaces have dried and no residue remains. If using chemical cleaners is a concern for you, try cleaning with non-toxic substances such as vinegar or baking soda.

Mothballs are poisonous to your cat. If you use them, keep them out of reach.

The taste and smell of antifreeze appeal to cats, but antifreeze contains ethylene-glycol, which is lethal to felines. If you spill antifreeze, clean it up immediately or purchase the new pet-friendly, non-toxic brands.

Cats like to jump on things, and because they determine whether something is hot by smelling it first, they may jump on an oven door unaware. After removing something from the oven, close the door immediately to keep your cat from jumping on it and burning his paws. If you are cleaning the oven, keep the door closed to prevent your cat from walking in the chemical cleaner.

If your cat chews or accidentally claws an electrical wire, he can die of electric shock. Keep electrical wires hidden. If that is not entirely possible, purchase hard plastic wire camouflage strips available at hardware stores. The strips have a slit in one side in which to slide the wire. They are inexpensive, can be cut easily to any length, and are designed to run along baseboards or up the walls.

Human medicines are also poisonous to your cat. Keep all medicines, even the over-the-counter variety, out of your cat's reach. Do not give your cat a medicine intended for humans unless advised to do so by your veterinarian.

Miniblind cords and drapery pulls dangle and invite a cat to play. Unfortunately, a cat can become caught in them and accidentally hang himself. Cut cords back to prevent your cat from being caught.

Keep all sewing needles, pins, thread, coins and paperclips out of sight and out of your cat's mind. These items are easily swallowed and can become lodged in the cat's throat. Often, surgery is the only way to remove them.

If you have an aquarium, your cat will have hours of enjoyment watching the fish. Keep the aquarium hood on at all times to keep your mini-mariner from going off the deep end into the water.

Cats and December Holidays

The holidays are a time of excitement for you, but for your cat they can bring a host of new hazards to his environment. Purchasing and decorating an artificial Christmas tree will deter most cats from climbing the holiday masterpiece, but this plan is not foolproof. If you have a tree, anchor it to the ceiling to prevent your cat from knocking it over. Place breakable ornaments near the top of your tree and the more feline-friendly, fabric, wooden or otherwise unbreakable, ones on the lower branches.

> **POINSETTIAS**
>
> Once on the list of poisonous plants, poinsettias have recently been determined not to be a hazard to cats. To keep your holiday plants safe from your cat, suspend them in hanging planters and out of reach of your feline friend.

If kitty swallows metallic tinsel or angel hair (which is made of fiberglass), it can get caught in the intestines and cause damage. Avoid using either in any holiday decorations.

Tie up electrical cords from your tree or other holiday lights to prevent your cat from chewing or catching his claws on them and accidentally electrocuting himself.

Unaware, a cat may flick his tail into the flame of a burning candle and accidentally set himself and your home on fire. If you light candles during the holidays or at other times, shield them in glass chimneys.

Cats love to pounce on ribbon and wrapping paper. Keep your cat from chewing on holiday ribbon, and make sure you and your guests don't step on kitty if he's hiding under the discarded package wrappings.

When You Are Away

When you go away on vacation or business, make sure that someone looks after your cat. A cat could have an accident even if you are gone only overnight, and treating the problem immediately could save his life.

Many veterinarians offer boarding facilities, if you would prefer to board your cat while you are gone. The benefits of boarding your cat at a veterinarian's office or reputable boarding facility are that someone will be there for most of the day to look after him. The downside is that your cat will be forced to remain in a small cage for an inordinate amount of time while you are gone, be near animals who may have contagious conditions such as respiratory infections and may have to listen to dogs barking and yowling. As a general rule, boarding a cat can be stressful and make him more susceptible to contracting illnesses.

Another option, if you do not have a friend whom you can trust or one who is able to care for your cat, is to hire a pet sitter to come once or twice a day to feed your cat and make sure he has not come to any harm. A pet sitter will also bring in your mail and water your plants if you desire. Your cat will be able to remain in his home environment, where he is most comfortable. If you hire a pet sitter, find one who has experience with cats and who is bonded. To find one near you, contact the Pet Sitters International Referral Hotline (see Chapter 14, "Resources").

Cats and Children

One of the greatest gifts a parent can give a child is a respect and reverence for other living things. Cats make wonderful pets for children and can get along quite well with them if the child learns at the start to handle the cat with care. Cats are smaller and more delicate than dogs. They do not tolerate or withstand rough-housing, preferring more gentle treatment such as stroking and petting. If you have a young child, teach him or her to handle your cat carefully and gently to help ensure that the two of them become friends.

chapter 6

Feeding

Your Cat

Providing your cat with a varied, nutritionally balanced diet and fresh water every day will help her maintain good physical and mental health and stay fit, alert and energetic. Proper nutrition will enhance your cat's appearance and make her coat shiny.

Americans spend more than $3.5 billion a year on cat food. As a result, cat food manufacturers spend a great deal of money and effort researching cats' nutritional requirements and taste preferences. A quick scan of the pet-food aisle in a grocery store will tell you that choosing food for your cat can be a complicated decision. Cat food is available in dozens of flavors. Some are formulated to meet cats' needs at the various stages of her life—from kittenhood, through adulthood to old age. Others are low-fat or light formulas for cats who need to lose a few pounds, or formulas to prevent or control common diet-related health problems. Add to that the premium foods available in pet stores and from veterinarians, and the task can seem overwhelming.

You may have to experiment with different types and brands of nutritionally balanced foods to see which one your cat likes best.

Complicating the decision about what types of food to buy are your cat's personal preferences. Cats have a reputation for being finicky, and given the same food more than once, they may devour it one time and ignore it the next. You may have to experiment with brands and flavors of food to find those your cat likes and provide her with a variety of nutritionally balanced food to keep her satisfied.

Your Cat's Nutritional Needs

To maintain good health, your cat needs food with adequate amounts of protein, vitamins, minerals, fats and carbohydrates. Unlike dogs, who can live on a vegetarian diet, your cat's metabolism requires a diet rich in animal protein and fat.

Protein provides your cat with energy and is the major structural component of hair, skin, nails, tendons, ligaments and cartilage. Protein is the major source of amino acids, which build new cells in muscle, bone and organ tissue. A cat's protein should come from a combination of meat, fish, poultry and eggs, to avoid dietary deficiencies from eating only red meat.

Dietary fat supplies cats with fuel for energy and fatty acids to carry vitamins where they are needed. Fatty deposits under the skin and around organs supply energy, protect the body from heat loss and provide a protective layer around organs to guard them against physical injury. Fat is often added to cat food to make it more palatable to their tastebuds.

Carbohydrates include starches and sugars. They are an energy source for tissue cells and ensure the proper functioning of the central nervous system and gastrointestinal tract. Although cats can exist adequately by consuming fats and protein as their sole energy sources, added carbohydrates in their diet will free the protein to be used for tissue repair instead of energy production.

Cats need protein, fats, carbohydrates and vitamins to remain healthy.

Your cat's food must also contain minerals to build body tissue. Minerals are inorganic elements that are essential for your cat's body processes. Calcium and phosphorus contribute to the growth and strength of bones and teeth, blood clotting and other metabolic processes. Magnesium aids metabolism and bone growth. Other minerals required in your cat's diet include potassium, sodium and chloride, iron and copper, zinc, manganese, cobalt and iodine.

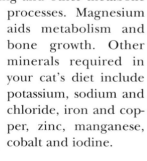

Vitamins are organic compounds that your cat requires for growth and maintenance of good health. Vitamins are either fat soluble, which means that they can be stored in body tissue, or water soluble, which means that excess amounts are passed

during normal waste elimination. Vitamins A, D, E and K are fat soluble, and therefore it is possible for a cat to experience problems due to consuming excessive amounts, just as it is possible to develop problems from too little. Water-soluble vitamins include B-complex and C and are necessary for energy metabolism, tissue synthesis and proper bone formation.

Many cat owners feel that they should give their cats vitamin supplements in addition to their regular diet. If you are feeding your cat food that is nutritionally balanced, dietary supplements are unnecessary. As your cat ages, however, she may develop conditions such as anemia that require the addition of supplements in her diet. Discuss your cat's needs for supplements with your veterinarian at her annual checkup.

Cat Food Labels and Contents

The contents of pet food and format of their labels are regulated by the Association of American Feed Control Officials (AAFCO), an organization of volunteer officials from state government bodies that regulates the production, labeling, sale and distribution of animal feed. The purpose of the AAFCO regulations is to standardize animal feed labeling from state to state so that a consumer can depend on the food's contents and nutritional value. So much information is packed into a pet food label that you may need a magnifying glass to read it.

Label Format   Every pet food label must contain the product name and brand, its net weight, directions for feeding, its guaranteed analysis, ingredients, and manufacturer's name and address. In addition, the label must indicate that the method used to substantiate the food's nutritional adequacy claim was in accordance with AAFCO procedures.

Guaranteed analysis   The amounts of crude protein, crude fat, crude fiber, and moisture must be listed as percentages and in that sequence. The term "crude," when applied to these nutrients, refers to the analytical procedures used to estimate their quantities in food. In addition, labels must contain the percentages of minerals such as calcium, phosphorus, and salt, as well as the amino acid taurine and ash, which is the resulting noncombustible materials in pet food after processing. Its primary content is magnesium. Although most cat food that is high in ash is also high in magnesium, a low-ash food is not necessarily low in magnesium. Ash content should not be used to measure a cat food's magnesium content.

Ingredients This part of the label lists, in descending order from the highest to lowest quantities, the contents of the food. The primary source of the protein content, such as liver, chicken or meat, is listed first. If the food is canned, it will consist of large quantities of water. The amount of water in a pet food cannot exceed seventy-eight percent. Water is usually followed by secondary protein and fat sources such as meat or poultry by-products, digest or grain. By-products are the clean portions of a food source stripped of its meat, which may include bone, heads, feet and viscera. Digest refers to the process of subjecting food parts to prolonged heat and moisture.

Additives Many cat foods contain added ingredients to enhance their color, flavor and aroma. Artificial color must be approved by the U.S. Department of Agriculture, and it is added to appeal to the pet owner rather than to the pet. Flavor enhancers must be approved by the Food and Drug Administration. Common flavor enhancers are onion and garlic powder.

Preservatives Added preservatives prevent food from oxidizing and therefore spoiling. Antioxidants are found naturally in grains and vegetable oils. Vitamins E and C are natural antioxidants. Synthetic preservatives include butylated hydroxyanisole (BHA) and butylated hydroxytoluene (BHT).

What Type of Food to Feed Your Cat

Cat food comes in three types: canned, semimoist and dry. Canned food comes in several sizes, from the 3.5-ounce gourmet variety to the large 14-ounce economy size, and is slightly more expensive than either semimoist or dry. A cat should not eat an entire can at one meal, so the unused portion must be refrigerated. Cats typically find canned food more palatable than dry or semimoist.

On the other hand, many cat owners find semimoist food more appealing to their own sense of smell than canned food, although good-quality and fishless varieties of canned food are not offensive to the nose.

How much and what kind of food you feed your cat should take into account health problems, activity level and individual tastes.

Dry food has several advantages to the cat owner as well as to the cat. It is less expensive than canned or semimoist cat food and convenient because it can be left out longer with little deterioration. Also, chewing dry food helps prevent the buildup of tartar on teeth.

Dry food, however, due to the higher magnesium content and reduced moisture, may contribute to a cat developing feline urologic syndrome (FUS), which contributes to the formation of crystals in the urinary tract and leads to obstruction of the urethra, a life-threatening condition.

There are many good, nutritionally balanced cat foods on the market, but you may want to discuss with your veterinarian buying premium food for your cat. Available canned or dry, premium foods have been developed to prevent health problems in cats. Much has been written about the merits of each type of food and whether cats need a variety of flavors or types. Some experts believe that if a food is nutritionally balanced, a cat can eat it exclusively and maintain good health. Others think that for good physical health and emotional well-being, a cat should have variety in her diet. Veterinary medical research is an ongoing process, and new findings about cats' dietary needs are continually being discovered, but you may want to try feeding your cat a variety of foods rather than counting on just one to be complete.

In addition to commercially available and premium cat foods, formulas are available for cats with specific medical or dietary needs such as FUS, kidney disorders, obesity and diabetes. If your cat develops a problem in any of these areas, discuss with your veterinarian what foods are available that are specifically formulated for cats with these conditions.

TUNA FISH

Tuna fish has a strong odor and smell that many cats find appealing. Feeding a cat large quantities of tuna can cause steatitis, a condition in which vitamin E is destroyed by excessive amounts of fatty acids such as those contained in red tuna meat. Feeding your cat small amounts of tuna as a treat or an occasional meal is completely acceptable, but choose tuna that is packed in water instead of oil.

Many cats show interest in what their human companions are eating. Some cats, especially those who once were strays or ferals and accustomed to scavenging for their daily rations, may display unusual gastronomic tastes and enjoy eating what in feline terms are more exotic delicacies such as cantaloupe, spaghetti, yogurt, spinach or other vegetables.

Your cat may come to your table and beg for portions of your meal. If you do not object to sharing your food with your feline companion, then giving your cat table scraps is completely acceptable. Because human food is not formulated to a cat's nutritional needs, table scraps should comprise no more than fifteen percent of your cat's total food intake. If you give your cat table scraps, do not include chicken or turkey bones. They splinter and break and can become lodged in your cat's throat.

Although your cat may show an interest in eating raw meat, it contains disease-carrying bacteria and parasites. Toxoplasma gondii is a gastrointestinal parasite that causes toxoplasmosis. It is estimated that more than fifty percent of the population of the U.S. has come into contact with toxoplasmosis. While this disease usually is not harmful to cats or to humans, it *is* harmful to the human fetus of a woman has come into contact with it during pregnancy. To avoid such problems, don't feed your cat raw meat and, if you are pregnant, avoid contact with an infected cat's feces.

How Much to Feed

The correct amount of food to give your cat is determined by its caloric content relative to your cat's caloric needs. These are determined by the cat's size, her age and her activity level and can vary considerably from one cat to another. Adult cats can vary in size from five to twenty or more pounds without being considered under- or overweight. Most manufacturers recommend the amount to feed on their product labels, but these estimates are based on feeding your cat only that particular product. In addition, commercial cat foods tend to recommend higher feeding amounts than what is actually necessary. For example, a manufacturer may recommend one 5.5-ounce can per 7.5-pound cat per day. That quantity may be a little high, depending on your cat's activity level and age, and whether your cat is consuming dry food as well.

The calorie contents of commercial cat food is beginning to appear on the labels, but as a new cat owner, you need not get into the complex task of trying to determine your pet's daily caloric intake or expenditure. Feeding a cat two meals per day, one in the morning and one in the evening, of a quantity that maintains her optimum adult weight is sufficient. If you feed your cat dry food, one-fourth to one-half cup per meal twice a day should be adequate. Of the canned variety, try feeding one-half to one whole can of a 3.5-ounce can or one-fourth to one-half of a 5.5-ounce can per meal twice a day, depending on your cat's build. Try combinations of canned and dry to help your cat maintain a healthy weight. Discuss with your veterinarian what is an optimum weight for your individual cat. When feeding your cat the refrigerated portions, bring them to room temperature first to prevent digestive problems.

Drinking

Water is a component of all living things and is essential to your cat's growth and maintenance. Water is lost from a cat's body during normal waste elimination and perspiration, so replacement on a daily basis is essential to your cat's good health. Although water is present in cat food, your cat requires fresh water at all times for proper metabolism. Special conditions such as hot weather or illness will make a cat drink more than normal. Not every cat drinks the same amount of water, however, so observe closely to determine what is normal for your cat.

Many cats like to drink from a running faucet. While this method will not harm your cat, it should not be a replacement for leaving a bowl of fresh water for your cat to enjoy.

Cats also will occasionally drink from the standing water in the toilet. If you use an automatic toilet bowl cleaner, keep the toilet lid down at all times to prevent your cat from ingesting the chemical substance.

Throughout history, giving kitty a bowl of milk has been considered the correct way of providing her with nourishment. Once a kitten is weaned at about six weeks of age, she no longer has a need for milk. Many cats exhibit a

AUTOMATIC FEEDERS

In recent years, devices have come on the market called automatic feeders. They are designed to hold at least a pound of dry food and dispense the food as the cat eats from a dish at the bottom of the feeder. While this is convenient for the owner, the device has drawbacks.

Once a cat owner becomes accustomed to her cat feeding herself from the automatic feeder, the owner may forget about the cat's needs and not notice when the food has run out. Food left out for extended periods of time can become stale and unappealing. Allowed to eat dry food at will, a cat may overeat and develop urological problems. Depending on the design of the feeder, a cat can get her head stuck inside the device when trying to reach inside for more food once the dish is empty.

Providing a pet with fresh food and water daily is one of the responsibilities of ownership.

lactose intolerance and develop diarrhea or vomiting when given milk. If you would like to give your cat milk occasionally as a treat, provide her with a lactose-free variety available in the pet-food section of your grocery store.

Food Bowls and Water Dishes

Cat food bowls come in all sizes and types of materials. A cat's food dish need not be elaborate or expensive. Because most cats eat by licking the food with their tongues rather than by lifting up chunks with their teeth, the food dish should have slightly curved sides so the food does not slide out onto the floor as the

Food dishes can be all sizes, colors and materials and need not be expensive.

cat eats. It also should be wide enough that the cat can put her mouth and nose into the bowl without flattening her whiskers against her face.

Ants can seem to come out of the woodwork to attack your cat's food and carry it away. To keep your cat's food from becoming infested with ants, sit the food dish inside a saucer of water. Ants cannot swim and will not cross the water to get to the food.

Feed your cat in a place that is convenient for you and comfortable for your cat. A corner of the kitchen that is out of the flow of traffic should work for both of you. Even if your cat goes outside, feed her indoors to avoid food being spoiled in the sun or attracting insects or rodents.

A water dish should be heavy enough to prevent it from tipping over. Some cats do not like to have their water dish near their food dish, so you may have to experiment to find a place where your cat will like to drink.

Food and water dishes should be washed daily. Some of the plastic twin dishes have removable bowls to make cleaning easier.

Dietary Disorders

"You are what you eat" is an adage that has been applied to humans and their eating habits, but it applies to your cat as well. Too much of some dietary substances or too little of others can contribute to certain health problems. Disease, age, temperament, heredity and environmental factors, such as stress or hot weather, can contribute to how well or how poorly your cat metabolizes her nutrients. In addition, certain foods may cause your cat to have allergic reactions.

KITTY ACNE

Cats can develop a skin condition known as feline acne. It is not the same as acne in humans, but most likely occurs due to their inability to wash their chins adequately after eating. Feline acne appears as a black, crusty formation on the chin. If left untreated, it hardens and becomes uncomfortable for the cat. As the cat scratches, the area becomes red and swollen and may bleed. Using plastic food bowls, which retain oils, can exacerbate the condition.

Treatment requires regular cleaning with mild soap and water. More serious conditions should be seen and treated by a veterinarian. To help prevent this condition, use glass or ceramic food bowls and wash them daily.

OBESITY

One of the most common dietary ailments experienced by cats is obesity. Unless a cat suffers from a metabolic disorder such as hypothyroidism, a cat becomes obese when the caloric intake is greater than the caloric expenditure, or when she eats too much and exercises too little. To keep your feline from becoming too fluffy around the middle, control her eating habits. To reduce a tubby tabby, try cat food that is lower in fat.

SKIN AND HAIR PROBLEMS

Skin and hair problems from a dietary source can be caused by a lot of different conditions, such as fatty acid deficiency or food allergies and sensitivities. Fatty acid deficiency can occur if a cat's food has been kept too long and become rancid. Cats fed a diet of people food often experience this problem. Dyes or additives may cause a cat to develop a form of dermatitis that results in severe itching or hair loss. Finding the dietary source of the allergy can be difficult. If your cat develops skin conditions, discuss the problem with your veterinarian and try feeding your cat with one of the hypoallergenic formula foods with a lamb, rabbit or venison base.

TAURINE DEFICIENCY

Lack of enough of this amino acid can cause the heart disease called dilated cardiomyopathy, and some degenerative retinal diseases. Most commercial cat foods have adequate levels of taurine.

FELINE UROLOGIC SYNDROME

Too much magnesium in your cat's food can contribute to feline urologic syndrome and the development of crystals in your cat's urine. When crystals build up, they can block the urinary tract and prevent your cat from urinating. Untreated, urinary blockage is fatal. Foods specially formulated to address FUS have lower magnesium levels and help prevent your cat from developing this problem.

chapter 7

Grooming
Your
Shorthaired Cat

Next to eating, sleeping and playing, one of your cat's favorite activities is grooming himself. Cats have a reputation for cleanliness and spend up to half of their waking hours performing this function.

A cat grooms primarily by licking his body with his rough tongue, which is covered by papillae, tiny projections that point backwards and help a cat remove dirt from his coat. These projections are what give your cat's tongue a rough feel.

We observe cats grooming most often following a meal or before sleep. Typically a cat will lick his paws and rub the dampened paw over his face, whiskers and chin to clean himself after eating. You may see your cat do what appears to be rapid biting in one spot as he washes. This stimulates the flow of saliva to aid in the grooming process. For debris that is difficult to remove or in a spot that is hard to lick, such as between the toes, a cat will pull or bite it off with his teeth.

Grooming has other functions besides keeping a cat clean and ensuring a soft, silky, shiny coat. It also removes dead hair and skin and stimulates the circulation of blood. In multicat environments, grooming is a social activity performed between cats, usually in the same family, or between cats who have formed a social bond.

Your cat will take care of most of his grooming needs but will require periodic assistance from you. The grooming process, if performed on a regular basis, will help your cat become accustomed to being handled, keep down the level of loose hair in your home, promote a good skin condition and prevent the spread of parasites, such as ear mites and fleas.

Most cats like to be combed and brushed. Other grooming activities occasionally are met with mixed reviews. To help your cat enjoy his grooming sessions, make the experience a pleasant one. Choose a location that has no distractions and one in which your cat likes to be. Make your cat comfortable by stroking and talking to him. The sound of your voice will help your cat enjoy and look forward to his grooming sessions.

Outdoor cats are more prone to fleas and other parasites, but indoor cats are not totally immune.

Part of the grooming process should be to examine your cat's ears, eyes, mouth and coat for any potential health problems or infestations of parasites. Finding problems early will prevent them from developing into more serious conditions.

Ears

Examine the inside of the ears. If your cat's ears are healthy, they will be pink and clean. If you see a black or dark brown substance that resembles soil in your cat's ears, it is a sign that the cat has mites. Cats with ear mites also shake their heads frequently and paw at their ears.

Outdoor cats are more likely to contract ear mites than those kept indoors. If you detect mites, have your cat examined by a veterinarian who will prescribe medication to kill the parasites. Treatment may take several weeks until all of the adults and eggs are eliminated.

Eyes

Your cat's eyes are protected by the eyelid and an inner lid that is found at the inner corner of the eye. If infected or inflamed, the inner lid may be exposed and red. This may be a sign that your cat has contracted an infection such as conjunctivitis. Such conditions can be treated and should be seen immediately by a veterinarian.

Some cats have a chronic or an occasional buildup of dirt in the corner of the eye. Simply remove it by wiping with a soft cloth. Tearing may mean that your cat has a piece of dirt or dust in his eye or has scratched it. Usually this will clear up within a day. If tearing occurs for longer periods, have your cat examined by your veterinarian.

Mouth

Examine your cat's teeth and gums. Brushing your cat's teeth will help prevent the buildup of tartar, but many cats resist this treatment. If you would like to try brushing your cat's teeth, discuss it with your veterinarian and ask him or her to recommend a specially designed brush and feline toothpaste. Do not use toothpaste intended for humans on your cat.

If you detect tartar buildup or reddened gums, have your cat examined by your veterinarian, who will be able to scale off some of the tartar. More serious buildup may require complete teeth cleaning, which is performed under anesthesia.

Coat

Your cat's coat should be clean and shiny. Although shedding hair is normal, stress or warm weather may make your cat shed more, and illness may make your cat less interested in grooming himself. If he has a skin condition or allergy, he may lick himself more, even creating bald patches.

Examine your cat's coat during normal grooming sessions. Are there signs of parasites? Are there any skin conditions that require medical attention?

FINDING AND FIGHTING FLEAS

The most common parasite to attack cats is the flea. If your cat has fleas, you will notice a substance that looks like salt and pepper in your cat's coat before you ever see a flea. The substance is a mixture of the undigested blood and flea droppings. Cats who spend time outdoors are prime targets for flea infestations. Once on the cat, the fleas come indoors when the cat does. Left untreated, fleas will infest your carpet, furniture and bedding.

Check your cat's teeth for tartar buildup.

Cats who have fleas will scratch excessively and may develop skin conditions, allergies and tapeworms. A tapeworm while in a cat's body is long and flat. Once tapeworms exit the body, they begin to curl up and die. You will recognize whether your cat has tapeworms by the small, ricelike particles around your cat's anal area. Once a cat contracts tapeworms, he may begin to loose weight.

Keeping a cat indoors, however, is no guarantee that he will be flealess. In order to eliminate fleas completely, you must not only eliminate them from your cat but from your home as well. Treating your cat with a flea product or dipping will have no effect if your cat comes home to a flea-infested house. Because fleas, eggs and larva can live up to two years in a home, you must kill the fleas in every life cycle, from egg to adult.

CAUTION

Regardless of the flea product you use, read the label carefully. Do not mix products on your cat. If you notice any symptoms such as excessive salivation or drooling, tremors, difficulty breathing or wobbliness, rinse the product off immediately and take your cat to a veterinarian.

Many types of flea shampoo for your cat and chemicals for the home exist. Before selecting any of them, discuss the situation with your veterinarian. He or she will be able to recommend products to you, and if you choose to go the route of dipping your cat to destroy the fleas, will be able to perform the procedure. Other products are available for cats as well, such as flea powders, sprays and flea-wipes—a disposable cloth similar to Handy Wipes™ for humans.

You may want to have your cat wear a flea collar. Flea collars come in many varieties and types and are specially treated to repel fleas before they attack your cat. Some flea collars come treated with natural, herbal flea repellents. Your veterinarian may keep a stock of flea collars or shop for one at a local pet store.

Products for the home vary in strength, length of effectiveness and potential harmfulness to people, pets and plants. Foggers are effective, but while using them, you, your cat, and every other living thing in your home, including plants, must be evacuated. Premise sprays can be used on carpets and furniture. Until the surface that has been sprayed dries, which takes three to four hours, your cat cannot walk on the area. The advantage over foggers is that you do not need to leave your home. While some are harmful to touch, they may not be harmful to breathe. You can do one room at a time and move your pet to another room while one is being treated. Both methods may require several applications before fleas in all life cycles are eliminated.

Though a cat cleans himself daily, certain conditions such as fleas or skin allergies can necessitate a bath.

OTHER PROBLEMS

During grooming be aware of other problems your cat may have. Cats are also susceptible to ticks, which burrow into the hair and skin and suck blood. When removing a tick, use flat-tipped tweezers and be sure to remove the entire tick. Deer ticks are known to carry lyme disease, and if your cat goes outside, he is more likely to encounter them. Cats that stay indoors are not at risk from ticks.

Ringworm is really not a parasite but a fungal infection of the skin. Ringworm develops into a small, circular area that has a crusty outer edge, and results in hair loss around the infected area. Ringworm is highly contagious and can be transmitted from human to cat and vice versa. Ringworm can be treated with antifungal medication. An infected cat should not be allowed to come into contact with other cats. Areas of the home that he comes into contact with should be disinfected with alcohol or diluted chlorine bleach.

BRUSHING AND COMBING

Brushing your cat with a soft natural-bristle brush will remove excess hair and stimulate the flow of oils to his coat. You should brush your cat at least once a week, and more often if he is shedding. A shorthaired cat is easier to brush and comb than a longhaired cat, but some shorthaired breeds have a double-coat that requires extra effort to keep the hair from matting and knotting. For this type of cat, an undercoat rake will help remove dead hair and keep the coat as knot-free as the outer coat. If necessary, use grooming shears designed to thin a cat's thick undercoat.

Most cats like to be combed and brushed, and grooming sessions can be made more enjoyable by stroking and gently talking to your cat.

Gently run a slicker brush along the cat's coat in the direction the hair grows, to remove dead skin. Be careful not to press so hard as to scrape the skin or break it open. When finished, brush your cat with the natural-bristle brush, to distribute oils through his coat and make it shiny.

If your cat is skittish about being groomed, try initiating him by using a grooming glove. A grooming glove fits over your hand and has small, rubber protrusions that remove dead hair as you stroke your cat. These are particularly helpful if your cat vanishes when he sees you approach wielding a brush. Stroking your cat with a grooming glove will remove excess hair and help your cat relax until you can graduate to other more effective grooming tools.

A fine-toothed comb, sometimes called a flea comb, will help remove dead skin and crusty areas that may occur around the eyes or on the chin and to carefully remove any knots that develop in your cat's coat. Flea combs can be safely used to remove fleas on your cat; they become trapped in the teeth of the comb.

Although not intended to replace regular grooming sessions with you, a corner comber is a device that will help your cat groom himself on a daily basis. A corner comber is made of hard plastic and attaches by screws to the corner of a wall or doorway in your home. It has tiny plastic teeth that, when kitty rubs against them, remove dead hair and smooth his coat. Install one and watch your cat comb himself each time he enters the room.

HAIRBALLS

Regular brushing and combing will help prevent your cat from developing hairballs. The hair your cat swallows when he washes can build up in his stomach or intestines. A cat who has hairballs will vomit them up generally, but if they have become lodged in his intestines, surgery may be required to remove them.

If your cat develops hairballs in spite of your good grooming efforts, give him a hairball remedy. Commercially available remedies come in regular and fish flavors to make them more appealing to kitty's tastes. Ask your veterinarian for a recommendation, or shop for one in a pet store.

Some cats do not like the flavor of hairball remedies and may opt for your jar of Vaseline, which is completely harmless for them to ingest in small quantities.

Clipping Claws

Claw clipping is an important part of the grooming process that will not only make your cat more comfortable but also help prevent damage to your furniture. Examine your cat's claws during your weekly grooming session, although you may not have to trim them each time.

To clip your cat's claws, use a clipper specially designed for cats. Gently spread the cat's paws so that the claws are distended. Insert the claw into the clipper and press the handle. When clipping, be sure to cut off only the tip of the claw, approximately one-eighth inch, and not the quick, which will bleed if cut and be painful for your cat. On most cats, the quick is easy to see: It is a pinkish area running along the top of the claw.

Bathing

Because cats wash themselves many times during the day, many pet owners and animal experts feel that there is no need to bathe them. Many cats do not like water, and, for them, the bathing process can be traumatic. Some conditions, such as fleas or skin allergies, however, can necessitate that you bathe your cat on occasion.

Fill the sink in which you are going to give your cat his bath with a few inches of water. Put a towel or rubber mat on the bottom to keep your cat from slipping. If you prefer, place a screen over the sink for your cat to sit on and hold onto with his claws. As you bathe and rinse, the water will fall below, eliminating the need for your cat to stand in water.

Use only a shampoo that is intended for cats. Shampoos for humans or for dogs can be toxic to your cat. If the dog shampoo contains flea-fighting insecticides for a large-size dog, the shampoo can be lethal. Once your cat is wet, massage the shampoo into the coat, being careful not to get it into the cat's eyes, nose or mouth. Using a spray hose or plastic cup, rinse the shampoo out of your cat's hair. Dry your cat with a towel or a blow dryer on the most gentle setting.

If you want to bathe your cat but he will not tolerate water, try using a dry shampoo. A pet store will have a selection. If you simply want to remove some odor that your cat may have picked up from the sides of his litter box, rub some baking soda into his hair, then brush it out to leave your cat's coat smelling clean.

Finding a Groomer

If you would like your cat to be groomed by a professional, find one who has been trained to groom cats. A cat groomer will know how to handle cats and be familiar with cat-grooming products. He or she will be sensitive to your cat's needs and be able to spot any potential problems, such as skin allergies, ear mites or mouth problems.

chapter 8

Your **Cat's** **Physical** **Health**

Thanks to advances in feline nutrition and veterinary medicine, cats are living longer than ever. The average lifespan of a cat is fourteen years. That's almost double what it was twenty-five years ago. With proper veterinary medical care, you can help ensure that you and your cat spend many years together.

Preventive Health Care

It is more humane and beneficial to your cat and easier and more cost effective for you to prevent health problems in your cat than to treat them once they occur. Providing your cat with regular exams and annual veterinary checkups is one of your responsibilities as a cat owner, and it will increase the length and quality of your cat's life. Regular checkups will help prevent problems before they start or become costly to treat— or untreatable altogether.

Your cat should see a veterinarian once a year for a complete physical exam and vaccinations. A veterinarian will be able to detect any problems or diseases early and recommend treatment to prevent their spread. He or she will perform a fecal examination to detect internal parasites.

VACCINATIONS

As part of your cat's annual checkup, your veterinarian will administer vaccinations against common feline diseases. The vaccine to prevent feline distemper, commonly called pan-leukopenia virus or FPV, is really a combination of three vaccines that provides protection against distemper, feline calicivirus and feline herpesvirus. Most veterinarians administer this vaccine annually.

Feline distemper is a highly contagious viral disease in cats. Although it can affect cats of all ages, it is most commonly a disease of kittens. Transmission of FPV occurs by direct contact with infected cats or with contaminated objects such as food bowls, litter pans or bedding. It also may be transmitted in its most acute stage by fleas. Vaccinating your cat against feline distemper will prevent her from contracting the disease.

Kittens need to be vaccinated against diseases, including feline distemper, which most commonly attacks young cats.

Feline calicivirus and **feline herpesvirus** cause acute respiratory infections in cats. Respiratory infections are highly contagious and, because they are airborne viruses, can be transmitted without direct contact with an infected cat. Respiratory infections can be treated with antibiotics, but annual vaccination against these conditions will prevent your cat from contracting the more contagious and dangerous respiratory diseases.

Rabies is a zoonotic virus that attacks the central nervous system of warm-blooded animals. Rabies is transmitted through a bite from a rabid animal or infected saliva entering the body through an open wound or through the eyes or mouth. Although treatment is available, it must be treated early. If it is not, the end result of rabies infection is death.

Rabies can be prevented through vaccination. Many states and municipalities have laws requiring that all pets be vaccinated against rabies annually. To prevent infection, have your cat vaccinated annually against this life-threatening disease.

HOME HEALTH EXAMS

It is important for you to give your cat a home health exam between her annual checkups. Your cat's general appearance and behavior offer clues about her health. Observing your cat on an ongoing basis will tell you when something is wrong. Early detection of a problem will aid in its treatment and prevent it from becoming more serious.

An annual trip to the vet can help prevent painful and costly health problems from developing.

Know your cat's vital signs. A cat's pulse rate is one hundred sixty to two hundred forty beats per minute. Your vet will measure your cat's pulse with a stethoscope, but you can obtain her heart rate by feeling directly on the chest just behind the foreleg. Once you feel the pulse, count the number of beats per minute.

Your cat's normal body temperature is between 100.4 and 102.5 degrees Fahrenheit. To take your cat's temperature, you will need a rectal thermometer. Before taking your cat's temperature at home, ask your veterinarian to show you how.

Lubricate the tip of the thermometer with petroleum jelly for easier insertion. Slide the thermometer into the rectum no more than one inch. Keep it inside for two minutes before taking a reading.

A cat's respiration rate is twenty to thirty breaths per minute. To measure her respiration, count the number of times she inhales by observing her sides for one minute. Heavy exercise can cause the respiration rate to elevate, so measure your cat's respiration when she is resting.

Examine your cat's coat, eyes, ears and mouth as part of her regular grooming sessions, as discussed in Chapter 7. You should point out any abnormalities to your veterinarian.

When Your Cat Gets Sick

Despite your good preventive health care, your cat may get sick from time to time. It is important for your cat's recovery that her environment be as stress-free as possible. Make sure that your cat stays in a room that is clean and warm. If your cat normally goes outside, keep her inside while she is convalescing.

Provide your cat with lots of fresh, cold water. If your cat has lost her appetite, offer her baby food in appealing flavors.

ADMINISTERING MEDICATION

If you must administer medication, ask your veterinarian to give it to you in a form that is easiest for you to give your cat. Medications come in pill or liquid form, and depending on your cat, one might be easier to administer than the other.

Liquid medication comes with a dropper and can be squirted into your cat's mouth. Some liquid medication can be mixed with your cat's food, but ask your veterinarian first whether this is acceptable for that particular medicine.

If you must pill your cat, grasp your cat's head above the jaws and tilt it back while pressing in with your forefinger and thumb. Push down the lower jaw with the forefinger of your other hand and drop the pill at the back of the tongue. If you have trouble pilling your cat, purchase a pill-gun, which will "shoot" the pill to the back of your cat's mouth. It is faster than trying to shove it back, and you don't risk your cat biting down on your finger. Once the pill is at the back of your cat's mouth, close her mouth and hold it shut until you see your cat swallow the pill. Many a clever cat has kept a pill in her mouth just long enough to fool her owner, only to spit it out when the owner walks away.

The Birds and Bees

Your cat will begin to experience a biological drive to reproduce once she has reached puberty. A female cat will go into heat, or "estrus," between the ages of seven and twelve months. Males usually reach puberty at nine months of age. Some purebred cats reach puberty at a later age than do random breeds. Cats who are kept indoors, especially if they are not housed with other cats, also may reach puberty at a later age.

For a cat owner, living with a cat in heat is a nerve-wracking ordeal. A female experiencing estrus will yowl, roll around, walk with her front end close to the ground and rear quarters raised, ready to receive a male even if none are available. She will rub against objects constantly and may mark them with urine to attract the feline Mr. Right. Females can exhibit this type of obnoxious behavior for months at a time, testing even the most patient and understanding owner.

A healthy cat will appear happy and alert.

Females can go in and out of heat constantly during the breeding season, which extends from January or February to September, and in that time period, can bear multiple litters of kittens.

Male cats spray a mixture of urine and anal-gland secretions to mark territory once they have reached puberty. Territorial marking will increase substantially in the presence of a female in heat, even if the female is outside of the home of an indoor male and vice versa. Spray from an intact male has an odor that can be detected easily by humans and cats alike.

Spaying and Neutering

An intact female cat is called a queen. Spaying, or ovariohysterectomy, is an operation performed under anesthesia to remove the ovaries, oviducts and uterus of an intact female. Cats who have been spayed may be required to remain in the veterinarian's office for one to three days following surgery. A spayed cat must return to the veterinarian for removal of stitches about ten days to two weeks later.

Neutering, also called castration, is a surgical procedure, performed under anesthesia, which consists of removing the testes of the male cat, or tom. Toms who have been neutered usually can return home the same day of their surgery. Neutering does not require stitches.

> **"ALTERING MAKES CATS FAT"**
>
> One of the myths surrounding the spay/neuter surgery is that once a cat is altered, she or he will become fat. Although altered cats may experience a drop in their energy levels, the only thing that will make a cat fat is overeating. To prevent cats from putting on pounds, monitor their food intake and make sure they get plenty of exercise.

Spaying or neutering, also called altering, is a proce-dure recommended by most veterinarians for any cat who is not part of a breeding program. The procedure generally is performed once the cat has reached six months of age, although veterinarians are altering cats at younger ages more frequently. It is preferable to per-form the surgery on a female before she has gone into heat and on a male before he has exhibited any terri-torial marking behavior.

Spaying and neutering are common surgeries and will provide your cat with several health and behavior benefits, as well as lifestyle benefits for you.

A spayed female is at less risk of reproductive disorders such as ovarian or mammary tumors and inflammation or infection of the uterus. She will not exhibit the behaviors associated with being in heat, and will be calmer and easier to live with.

EARLY WARNING SIGNS

Many problems and diseases in cats have similar symptoms. Diagnosis depends on your observing her carefully and providing your veterinarian with that information. Knowing when something is wrong with your cat first requires that you know how she acts under normal circumstances. Do certain foods cause her to have loose bowels or become constipated? Does she eat less in warm weather? Does she typically hide from strangers?

If your cat exhibits any of the following abnormal symptoms, something is wrong, and she should be seen by a veterinarian.

Blood in the stools or
   urine

Coughing

Diarrhea for more than
   one day

Gagging

Hair loss

Limping

Loss of appetite

Nasal discharge

Sudden aggressive or
   antisocial behavior

Tearing or cloudiness
   in one or both eyes

Weight loss or gain
   that is sudden

Wheezing

Neutering a male will significantly reduce the risk of territorial spraying. Studies have shown that ninety percent of neutered male cats do not spray. Of those who do, the sprayed substance looses its catty smell, and your home will not fall victim to telltale cat odors.

For a cat, reproduction is a biological function. Although a female who has given birth will protect her young, cats do not long to bear young or have even one litter of kittens. By spaying your cat, you will not be depriving her of the joy of motherhood. You will be making her a happier, healthier pet.

If your cat is male, neutering will not deprive him of a hot night on the town. Reproduction for a tom is instinctual and biologically, not emotionally, motivated.

Spaying and neutering are such important procedures that organizations have popped up all over the United States to offer low-cost spay/neuter surgery. Ask your vet about a low cost spay/ neuter programs

In addition to the benefits to your cat of having him or her neutered or spayed, you will be benefiting cats everywhere. The

Humane Society of the United States estimates that each year more than eight million dogs and cats are put to death in shelters across the United States because there are not enough homes for them. More suffer and die, alone and unwanted on the streets. For every cat who is brought into the world by a well-intentioned owner, one dies homeless in a shelter somewhere. By altering your cat, you will be preventing the births of more kittens in a world already overcrowded with them.

Viral Diseases

A major threat to your cat's good health and physical well-being is potential infection from viruses. A virus consists of nucleic acid surrounded by a protein coat. They are not living organisms, but instead rely on living cells as hosts to reproduce. Some viruses can remain dormant and have no affect on the living host. Others may produce a response by the host's immune system that is more serious than the virus itself. Viruses do not respond to antibiotics, and often the only method of treatment is to address secondary symptoms of the infection.

FELINE LEUKEMIA VIRUS

Feline Leukemia Virus, or FeLV, was first discovered in 1964. FeLV is transmitted primarily through infected saliva from bite wounds or grooming, but it also can be spread to cats who share litter boxes and food bowls or in utero from an infected mother to her kittens. Cats at the highest risk of contracting FeLV are those living in multicat environments who engage in social grooming of one another and share food bowls and litter pans. Cats who spend time outdoors, especially toms fighting over females, are at risk from infected free-roaming cats.

The feline leukemia virus is not an airborne virus. It is weak and does not survive more than a few hours outside the body. If you come into contact with a feline leukemia–positive cat outside or at a shelter, for example, you will not carry the virus home on your clothes.

Feline leukemia produces different reactions in different cats. Approximately forty percent of the cats who come into contact with FeLV develop immunity and shed the virus. The remainder become either carriers with no visible symptoms or develop symptoms characteristic of the disease. Of the cats who are latent carriers, most have no visible signs of the disease and go on to live normal lives, yet will pass the virus on to their offspring. Stress or poor diet, which weakens a cat's immune system, may eventually cause the virus to resurface. Cats who develop symptoms of the disease may live anywhere from three months to three years, during which time they may infect any cat with whom they come into contact.

Cats who suffer from the full-blown leukemia infection may develop tumors or anemia, lose their blood-clotting ability or suffer from a total suppression of their immune system. Immune suppression makes it difficult for them to fight off infections such as pneumonia, respiratory problems, skin and mouth infections and stomach problems.

No cure for feline leukemia exists. The only way to determine whether your cat has FeLV is to have her tested. If your cat's test comes back positive, wait six weeks and have her tested again. This allows enough time to determine whether your cat may shed the virus following contact. If your cat truly is feline leukemia positive, make her as comfortable as possible and watch her closely for signs of secondary infection. Keep her indoors and away from other cats.

FELINE LEUKEMIA VACCINES

The first feline leukemia vaccine was patented in 1985. Since then, new vaccines have come on the market of the live, modified live or killed virus type. They require differing initial dosages administered at several-week intervals, followed by annual boosters. Some can be given in combination with vaccinations against other preventable diseases.

If your cat has tested negative for feline leukemia, talk to your veterinarian about vaccinating your cat against the disease. Vaccination is especially important if your cat goes outside or if you are considering adding another cat to your household.

FELINE INFECTIOUS PERITONITIS

Feline Infectious Peritonitis (FIP) was first recognized in the early 1960s and can cause a broad spectrum of diseases that range from no symptoms at all to full-blown FIP. The FIP virus infects white blood cells that are part of a cat's immune system. The cells then transport the virus to many other parts of the body, where it causes an inflammatory reaction and tissue damage.

*Your veteri-
narian should
be knowledge-
able about cats,
trustworthy and
communicative.*

FIP most often attacks cats from six months to two years of age. It is significantly less common in cats than feline leukemia but quite serious to those infected. Although scientists are not sure how FIP is transmitted, they estimate that it is through ingestion or inhalation of the virus and that direct contact with an infected cat is not necessary. Infected cats may shed the virus through oral and nasal secretions, urine and feces.

Cats suffering from FIP show severe inflammation of the lining of the abdomen and its organs. Accumulation of fluid within the cat's abdomen or chest will cause it to swell significantly. Other symptoms include difficulty breathing, fever, listlessness and weight loss.

FIP is considered a fatal disease. Veterinarians treat an FIP-positive cat with antibiotics and immune-suppressing medications to fight secondary symptoms. If the cat still has an appetite and does not have another condition such as feline leukemia, FIP may go into temporary remission, but the long-term prognosis is fatal.

FELINE IMMUNODEFICIENCY VIRUS

Feline Immunodeficiency Virus (FIV) is the most recently discovered immunosuppressive virus and was first found in a colony of feral cats in California.

Exactly how FIV is transmitted is unknown, but scientists suspect bite wounds to be a primary vehicle. Following infection, FIV is carried to the lymph nodes, where it replicates in white blood cells. Eventually the cat's white blood count and red blood count will drop, and the cat will develop a fever. An FIV infected cat may live for years but eventually develops signs of immunodeficiency and is unable to protect itself from secondary infections.

Symptoms of FIV are difficult to isolate from those of other diseases but may involve chronic skin infections, urinary bladder and upper respiratory infections, diarrhea, seizures and other neurologic disorders. Treatment involves use of medications such as antibiotic or antifungal drugs to fight off secondary infections and supportive care such as intravenous fluids, blood transfusions or high-calorie dietary supplements.

No cure or vaccine exists for FIV. A veterinarian will be able to test your cat by using an FIV antibody test, but the best way to prevent your cat from contracting FIV is to keep her indoors.

FIP VACCINE

No cure exists for FIP, and tests cannot distinguish between types of coronaviruses, only one of which is FIP. A modified-live vaccine for FIP was developed in 1991. The vaccine is given in drops through the nose. Subsequent studies performed at the Cornell Feline Health Center have shown that the vaccine was not as protective as the original tests indicated and that cats who received the vaccine could become carriers of FIP and infect other cats.

If your cat does not go outside or come into contact with unfamiliar cats, vaccinating against FIP is not recommended.

Emergency First Aid

Even the most careful cat owner cannot totally eliminate from the home the threat of an accident. A cat
could fall and break a bone, tear a toenail by catching
it in carpet or fabric, cut herself on a sharp object or
experience some other catastrophe which will require
that you have a knowledge of first aid and how to handle emergencies.

If an accident happens, try to remain calm. Your cat's
well-being will depend on your acting quickly and
directly. Keep your veterinarian's telephone number
or that of an emergency clinic posted where you can
find it quickly if you need to. Also post the telephone
number of the nearest poison control center. The staff
there will tell you what to do if you suspect your cat has
ingested a poisonous substance.

Take a deep breath and determine what the problem
is. Check your cat's vital signs. Perform the necessary
stop-gap procedure until you can get your cat to a
veterinarian.

BLEEDING

Determine the severity and type of wound. A closed
wound is an abrasion or contusion and is less serious
than an open wound, which includes punctures, lacer-
ations and amputations. If the wound is a scratch or
scrape, clean it with three percent hydrogen peroxide
on a cotton ball or swab. Apply antibacterial ointment.

If the wound is more serious and there is significant
blood loss, apply direct pressure with a gauze pad.
Maintain pressure or wrap the wound in gauze tape
until you can get your cat to a veterinary clinic.

BREAKS

If your cat has a broken bone, try to keep her station-
ary. If your cat moves around, a simple fracture could
turn into a compound fracture—one in which the
bone protrudes from the skin. Place the cat gently into
a carrier or box and take her to your veterinarian as

quickly as possible. Do not try to apply a splint, as this will make the cat more uncomfortable and could cause more damage.

BURNS

The most common burns in cats are to the paw pads (when a cat jumps on a hot surface), or singed hair (for example, when a cat gets too close to a flame). Burns also can occur if the cat comes into contact with chemicals or electrical current. If it is a surface burn, rinse the area with cold water. If the burn is chemical, wear rubber gloves so that you don't burn your skin. Never apply creams or oils to a burn. Take your cat to a veterinary clinic as soon as possible.

FELINE AIDS

Feline Immunodeficiency Virus is often referred to as feline AIDS because it functions in cats the same way as AIDS, Acquired Immunodefiency Virus, functions in humans. Scientists have classified FIV in the same subfamily of viruses as the virus that causes progressive pneumonia in sheep, infectious anemia in horses, arthritis-encephalitis in goats and AIDS in humans.

Feline Immunodeficiency Virus is not the same thing as AIDS. FIV cannot be transmitted from a cat to a human, and AIDS cannot be transmitted from a human to a cat. If your cat is diagnosed with FIV, you cannot get AIDS from your cat.

CHOKING

A cat will choke on an object that has become lodged in her throat. She will exhibit signs of labored breathing, may paw at her mouth or gag. Hold your cat and open her mouth to remove the object. If it is too far back, perform the Heimlich maneuver by placing your cat on her side. Place one hand on her spine, and with your other hand, push down and forward behind the cat's rib cage several times. If you cannot remove the object or if your cat continues to have difficulty breathing once the object is removed, take her to a veterinary clinic.

ELECTRICAL SHOCK

Electrical shock from biting and chewing on electrical wires is a common problem among cats. Signs of electrical shock include burns around the mouth, convulsions, a respiration rate of less than ten breaths per minute, unconsciousness or no pulse. If your cat is still connected to the electrical wire, turn off the source of the power. Check your cat's vital signs. If she has a pulse, get her to a veterinarian immediately. If there is no pulse, perform cardiopulmonary resuscitation (CPR).

CPR

To begin, hold your cat steady with one hand. Place the thumb of your free hand on your cat's chest at the point of the elbow, and your fingers on the opposite side of the chest cavity for compression. Squeeze gently but firmly at a rate of one compression per second. After five compressions, follow with artificial breathing by opening your cat's mouth and pulling the tongue forward. Push down firmly on her ribs and release to drive stale air out of the lungs. Hold the cat's mouth closed, put your mouth over her nose and gently breathe into her nostrils for three seconds. Continue this procedure for up to thirty minutes or until your cat begins to breathe on her own.

POISONING

You can prevent accidental poisoning in your own home by keeping all dangerous chemicals and plants out of reach. If your cat goes outside, she runs a greater risk of being accidentally or intentionally poisoned. Symptoms of poisoning include vomiting, diarrhea, convulsions, weakness, drooling, irritations in the eyes or mouth and unusual or odorous substances on your cat's hair or skin.

If you suspect your cat has been poisoned, try to identify the substance. Give her activated charcoal tablets to absorb the poison, then call your local poison control center for additional instructions. Then get your cat to a veterinarian as quickly as possible.

Choosing the Right Vet

One of the most important things you will do for your cat is choose the right veterinarian. A good veterinarian who is knowledgeable about feline medicine and who understands and likes cats will help you make sure that your cat obtains the best available health care. Becoming a veterinarian requires at least seven years of college and post graduate schooling. Staying on top of the latest advances in veterinary medicine requires ongoing study and staying active in the profession. In addition, a veterinarian must be licensed to practice by the state in which he or she is located.

The primary factor to consider when choosing a veterinarian is trust. The AVMA estimates that more than 65,000 veterinarians are practicing in the U.S. While that is a lot to choose from, finding one who suits your needs and one with whom you can communicate may require that you shop around. You and your veterinarian will share in your cat's health and well-being for a very long time, so it is important that you are satisfied that the care your cat is receiving is the very best.

"CATS ALWAYS LAND ON THEIR FEET"

A popular myth that surrounds the domestic cat is that she always lands on her feet when she falls. While your cat may be able to experience some minor falls and still land on her feet, don't expect this to always happen. Cats often fall in ways that can cause physical harm. In addition, many cats die every year from "highrise syndrome," falling from windows in highrise apartments. Don't count on your cat surviving a fall. Keep windows and screens secure.

If you have friends who own cats, ask them to recommend a veterinarian. Ask what they like about their vet and what they might like to see improved.

When you arrive at the veterinarian's office for the first time, look around. The waiting room should be clean, neat and cheerful. There should be no remnants of kitty or doggie "accidents" on the floor. You should be able to wait for your appointment without having dogs running loose, barking or otherwise frightening your cat. Receptionists and technicians who register you should be friendly and helpful. They should obtain a full history of your cat on the first visit—her age, what she eats, what veterinarians she has seen and what medical problems she might have had.

A veterinarian should be willing to spend time with you explaining what he or she is doing and listening to you explain the symptoms you have observed in your cat. Does the veterinarian seemed hurried, or is he or she willing to listen as well as talk?

When visiting the veterinarian, your cat may appear timid or frightened. A veterinarian should be patient with your cat if she is afraid to come out of her carrier. He or she should be friendly toward you and your cat and should handle your cat firmly but gently.

Establishing and maintaining a good relationship with your veterinarian is a two-way street. As a client, you should expect certain things from your veterinarian, but he or she should also expect certain things from you:

1. Be respectful of your veterinarian's time. Do some homework before taking your cat for an exam. If your cat is experiencing problems, make a list of questions you want to ask and take them with you. If necessary, write down the answers your vet provides so that you do not have to ask the questions again.

2. Observe your cat's symptoms and be willing to describe her condition to your veterinarian.

3. Don't interpret your cat's symptoms. Let your veterinarian make the medical diagnosis of your cat's condition.

4. Your cat's health may depend on you following your veterinarian's instructions. If he or she tells you something that you do not understand or uses

---

MAKING A FIRST AID KIT

Keeping a well-stocked medicine cabinet will help you be prepared for an emergency. All of these items are available at drugstores or discount pharmacies. Do not give your cat milk of magnesia to treat poison or kaolin to treat diarrhea unless instructed to by your veterinarian or poison control center.

Supplies:

Blunt-end scissors

Flat-end tweezers

Gauze bandages,
1-inch and 3-inch rolls

Cotton swabs or balls

Rectal thermometer

Medications:

Antibacterial ointment

3 percent hydrogen peroxide

Milk of magnesia tablets

Activated charcoal tablets

Kaolin mixture

terminology that is new to you, ask him or her to explain it.

5. Pay your veterinarian for his or her services. If your cat requires costly treatment, discuss payment options. Nothing is sadder for a veterinarian to euthanize a cat at an owner's request simply because the owner could not afford the surgery. Your veterinarian should be able to work out payment arrangements with you for unusual circumstances or costly treatments.

Herbal medicine, acupuncture and homeopathy can be used with other remedies to treat feline illnesses.

Over the years, your cat may have medical problems that require emergency treatment. When choosing a veterinarian, ask what allowances he or she has made for after-hours care or situations that arise when he or she is on vacation. Are there other practitioners in the office who will examine your cat when your regular veterinarian is away? Will they see your cat after regular office hours, or do they have a clinic you can call in an emergency?

When you take your cat for an exam, make sure your veterinarian has indicated upfront what you will be charged. Discuss all vaccinations, medications and treatments so that you know why they are being recommended and what they will cost you. There should be no hidden fees for your veterinarian's services.

Other Kinds of Veterinary Services

The sight or sound of dogs can be traumatic to a cat, especially one who has never been around them. Unfortunately, your cat may have to deal with dogs every time she visits the vet, adding more stress to an already stressful situation.

If you would like to have your cat visit a veterinarian in a dog-free environment, choose a veterinarian who operates a practice devoted exclusively to cats. Veterinarians whose only clientele are of the feline variety are more sensitive to cats' needs. Because they specialize in one type of veterinary medicine, they are able to stay on top of the latest developments in feline medicine.

If you would like your cat to have her annual checkups and veterinary visits in the comfort of your home, find a veterinarian who will make house calls. Many veterinarians choose to see patients in their homes because the animal feels less stressed.

Care and treatment of the whole animal and not just specific symptoms is called holistic veterinary medicine. Once scorned by modern medical science, holistic medicine is experiencing a rebirth for animals as well as humans. Many veterinarians are combining holistic veterinary medicine with modern, conventional techniques such as surgery and pharmaceuticals.

> ## PET HEALTH INSURANCE
>
> More than forty percent of veterinary visits are for sudden illness or accidents. Diagnosis and treatment for a seriously ill cat or one who has been involved in an accident can exceed $2,500. Pet health insurance is available to help pet owners cover the costs of catastrophic illnesses or accidents. Pet health insurance usually does not cover the costs of routine exams or cosmetic or elective surgery such as spaying or neutering. The costs of such plans are based on the cat's age. They may have certain qualifiers and usually come with a deductible.
>
> If you are interested in health insurance for your cat, discuss it with your veterinarian, who will be able to refer you to providers.

Herbal medicine, homeopathy and acupuncture can be used to treat an animal solely or in conjunction with other types of veterinary procedures. Of the holistic techniques, acupuncture is to date the only one that has been officially recognized as a legitimate form of treatment by the American Veterinary Medical Association.

If you would like to learn more about holistic medicine or find a veterinarian trained in holistic techniques, contact the American Holistic Veterinary Medical Association. To find a veterinarian trained in acupuncture specifically, contact the International Veterinary Acupuncture Society (see Chapter 14, "Resources," for addresses of both organizations).

chapter 9

Your Cat's
Mental
Health

The cat inside your home has been domesticated for thousands of years, and although he still retains some of his wilder instincts, he will depend on you for his mental as well as physical health and emotional well-being. Talking to your cat, playing with him, and providing him with exercise, fresh air, sunshine, mental stimulation and a stress-free environment will help him stay mentally fit and alert and create a contented, happy housepet. Good mental health ultimately will contribute to your cat's physical health as well.

Play and Exercise

Most of nature's creatures have a need for play and engage in it when they are young. Who hasn't taken delight in watching baby animals romp with one another or torment their mothers in an attempt to lure them into games? Play and the invention of games help a young animal develop his instinctive behavior and prepare for life as an adult.

Your cat will play naturally when he is a kitten, but the need for play and exercise does not end there. Given proper stimulation, your cat will continue to play for most of his life and satisfy his need for exercise to keep fit and healthy.

Interactive cat toys are a good way to help your cat get plenty of exercise. There are many good toys on the market that require your cat to run, jump or climb while he plays. Several popular items resemble fishing poles and lines with feathers or swatches of fabric attached to the ends. Some have feathers that swirl when you swing them around. Others have satin cords attached to a sturdy Lucite handle. Each of these items is intended for you to play with your cat, and dragging the feathers around or swinging them through the air will entice your cat into a hunting or pouncing game.

ROTATING TOYS

Cats become bored and disinterested in their toys if they have access to them at all times. To keep kitty interested in his playthings and keep your expenses down, try rotating the toys periodically. When you purchase or make a new toy, put the old ones away for awhile. When your cat tires of his new toy, put it away and get out some of the older ones.

Because cats are curious animals and have an instinct to hunt, try hiding your cat's toys at various places around the house for him to find and play with when you are not at home.

When playing with any toy that has string, yarn or cords on it, be sure to put the toy away when you are finished. Some cats like to chew on string, and ingesting it can be harmful.

A recent entry into the cat toy market is a round plastic device with a Ping-Pong ball that rolls around inside it. Cats love to bat the ball inside the circular track, trying to get it out. Another popular item is a box with a Ping-Pong ball inside and holes on the sides for cats to reach inside and bat the ball.

Cats also enjoy toys made with catnip. Catnip is a member of the mint family, and cats are drawn to the smell.

Catnip toys are usually intended for the cat to play with by himself, and a selection of catnip toys will give your cat the opportunity to play while you are not at home. The catnip experience can last up to fifteen minutes. Cats vary in their reactions to catnip, from appearing mildly intoxicated to exhibiting wildly sensuous behavior similar to that of a female in heat. Some cats show no response, while others who can't seem to "hold their catnip" may become overly sensitized and react aggressively to human touch while "under the influence."

Kittens will play naturally, but older cats need the stimulation that play provides just as much.

Catnip is perfectly safe to give your cat. Fresh leaves are a little more potent than dried, but if your cat likes catnip, both varieties will elicit a response. Constant access to catnip causes it to lose its effect, so you may want to provide it only as a treat.

Other toys that interest felines can be made from swatches of fake fur or carpet cut in interesting shapes or molded around tubes that roll. A word of caution, however: Some toys on the market are not designed with your cat's safety in mind. Small bells, removable eyes, string or yarn parts are easily swallowed and can stick in your cat's throat. Before giving your cat a toy, remove any small, dangerous parts.

Indoor games and activities need not be complicated or even expensive. Using a little creativity and imagination, you can make many exercise devices or toys from things found around the house.

Crumpled paper Crumple a piece of paper and roll it for your cat to chase. Tie a piece of crumpled paper on the end of a string and drag it around for your cat to pounce on.

Boxes Cats love to get into boxes. Cut holes in a cardboard box for your cat to run in and out of. Place a cardboard flat from soda or food cans on the floor and watch your cat slide around in it.

Balls Place a Ping-Pong or practice golf ball inside a carton for your cat to pounce on. Roll one on the floor for it to chase. Bounce a one-inch rubber ball for your cat to jump and catch.

Paper grocery bags Put one on the floor and tap your fingers on the end. Watch as your cat pounces into and out of the bag.

Socks Stuff an old sock with catnip and tie a knot in the end.

Cats can have hours of fun playing in cardboard boxes.

Chapter 5 discussed the importance of scratch posts in helping your cat remove the old sheaths from his toenails and keeping him from clawing your furniture. The larger multilevel posts also provide your cat with places to climb, jump and just hang out when he wants to get away from it all. Multilevel posts make use of the vertical space inside the home and add to a cat's sense of adventure. This is a useful technique if you live in a small apartment or townhouse and want to increase the space available for your cat.

Multilevel cat posts are often fashioned with nooks and crannies, tubes or huts that function as feline hideaways or observation towers for a cat who wants to find a place to sleep or hide.

Your cat needs exercise, fresh air and sunshine for mental fitness.

Bringing the Outdoors in

Cats need fresh air and sunshine. Open windows bring in a world of new scents from the outside that will help keep kitty from succumbing to boredom. Sunlight, even what enters through open windows, is an excellent source of vitamin D. If you plan to keep your cat indoors, providing him with fresh air and sun may take some extra work on your part but will be well worth the effort for your cat's long-term well-being.

If you would like your indoor cat to enjoy the outdoors, purchase or build an outdoor enclosure or run that your cat can access through a pet door. Enclosures provide the cat with the benefits of outdoor living without the dangers. Make the enclosure more interesting by adding objects for your cat to explore. Tree limbs with attached platforms on which your cat can perch, tires or toys hanging from branches, and boxes in which your cat can curl up and hide make the enclosure more fun.

Fence systems are available that are designed to keep a cat from climbing over them and out of the yard. If you allow your cat outside into a fenced-in yard or enclosure, provide shelter from the hot sun or from inclement weather for your cat. Better yet, provide a pet door or way for him to come back inside at will. Also make sure that plenty of fresh water is available for your cat when he is outside in warm weather.

A less expensive way to provide your cat with fresh air and sun is to install perches at various windows around the house. Window perches come covered with carpet or soft, plush fabric, and cats love to sit on them and watch whatever comes by. Perches may require permanent installation on the window sill or come with Velcro and support bars for easy movement from one window to another.

Perches provide your cat with a window on the world. Try making the view more interesting by attaching Lucite bird feeders to the other side of the window or a free-standing or hanging bird feeder nearby.

Mental Stimulation

Cats have active minds as well as bodies, and providing mental exercise is as important to your cat's well-being as providing physical exercise. Lacking stimulation, a cat can become bored and listless, experience stress, become more susceptible to illness and, at the extreme, engage in self-mutilating activities such as chewing his tail.

STRESS INDUCERS

The following conditions may cause your cat to experience stress and, if not treated in time, may result in the development of secondary symptoms of illness:

Absence of his owner

Addition of another family member, pet or roommate

Animals, domestic or wild, congregating outside the home

Boredom

Changes in the status of the family or living group

Emotional state of his owner

Excessive cold

Excessive heat

Fleas or parasites

Illness

Inability to groom

Interpersonal problems among friends or family members

Loss of his owner, a family member or animal playmate

Moving to a new home

Noises

Traveling

Visiting the vet

Visitors to the home

One important way you can provide your cat with mental stimulation is by talking to him. Many people are uncomfortable or embarrassed by the thought of carrying on a conversation with kitty and fear being thought of as strange or outright crazy. But cats rely on the sound of their persons' voices and the words they use to learn new things, to determine what activities they are not allowed to do and to help them gauge their owners' dispositions. Cats respond to their owner's moods and emotional states, and they will provide comfort when their person is sad or unhappy, just as they will provide enjoyment and fun when the owner is not. Hearing you speak to him will increase your cat's comfort level, especially in stressful situations such as visiting the vet or getting a bath.

Keep your cat interested in his toys by rotating them periodically.

If cats can learn their names and even nicknames, it stands to reason that they also can learn other words and what they mean. Because cats have the ability to learn and respond to a great many words, human language will not go unnoticed or be wasted on your feline friend as long as it is simplified and looks at a situation from your cat's point of view. Just as a dog owner may get a dramatic, positive reaction when he says to his dog, "Let's go for a walk," you will get emotional responses from your cat if you speak to him and develop consistent ways of referring to the activities you engage in together. Using

113

language and conversation in this way will help you develop a closer relationship with your cat.

Cats also have the ability to see and respond to two-dimensional images, such as what is seen on a television screen. Some observant and entrepreneurial cat owners have capitalized on cats' ability and created videos designed to appeal to cats. Birds, squirrels and moving fish can engross a cat for fifteen to twenty minutes at a time. While you may not want your cat to become a couch potato, adding a little video time may enliven your cat on a dull or hot day.

The loss of an animal playmate can be extremely stressful for a cat.

Stressing the Impact of Stress

Cats are sensitive creatures and, like other animals, including humans, respond to stress. Cats can experience stress from a variety of stimuli, and often the source can be so subtle that it is difficult to detect. What constitutes a stressful condition may vary significantly from one cat to another. For some it may be moving to a new home, while for others it can simply be rearranging the living room furniture.

Symptoms of stress may include chronic illness, loss of appetite, hiding, skin disorders or even aggressive responses to humans or other animals. Every cat owner at one time or another experiences stress or must undergo changes in his or her lifestyle or environment. To keep your cat from reacting negatively to stressful situations, talk to him more during times of change; provide him with plenty of love and affection, places around the home to hide, and adequate care when you are away for more than a day; and monitor his health and outward appearance. Obtain veterinary care if necessary. Keeping a home that is as stress-free as possible will help your cat maintain optimum mental and physical condition.

Enjoying

Your

Cat

part three

chapter 10

Your
Cat's
Behavior

Watching cats interact with their world is one of the joys of living with them. "What is my cat doing?" or "Why is my cat doing that?" are two questions that cat owners ask over and over again. While some feline behaviors may forever remain a mystery, understanding as much as possible why your cat behaves as she does will help you communicate and strengthen the bond between you.

Keys to Communication

One of the primary ways cats express themselves is through body language. Posturing, facial expressions and tail movement all combine and contribute to letting a person or other animal know

118

what is on a cat's mind. By observing your cat closely, you will discover that she has the ability to experience a wide range of emotions and to communicate them to you.

BODY POSTURES

A happy, contented cat will walk with her head high, eyes straight ahead, and tail erect. A cat who is facing a rival will stand erect but with her head held low, sometimes angling it as she begins to yowl. The subordinate or frightened cat will crouch. A cat who is on the defensive may arch her back with her hair standing on end to make herself appear larger in the face of a perceived enemy. A cat who is uncertain or fearful of her environment may walk in a crouched position as she slowly investigates her surroundings.

FACIAL EXPRESSIONS

Observing a cat's ear positions, eye expressions, pupil dilation and facial muscle movements will provide you with additional clues about what your cat is thinking and feeling. The ears of a cat who is alert and happy will stand up straight. As she listens to sounds in her environment, the ears will move back and forth like a satellite dish moving to increase reception. A relaxed cat will have bright, clear eyes, with the pupils adjusted according to the amount of light present. If the surroundings are dark, the pupils will be dilated. If the area is bright, the pupils may close to the point of being slits down the center of the eyes.

If a cat experiences fear or is on the defensive against another animal, she will flatten her ears back against her head. This ear position is usually accompanied by increased pupil dilation and a gaping mouth. As a cat becomes more angry or aggressive, she will flatten her ears tightly against her head, open her mouth to bare her teeth, and constrict her facial muscles around her mouth and nose and on her forehead. This intense facial expression may be accompanied by hissing, spitting or even loud screaming to scare off an enemy.

A cat is curious about her environments and will use all her senses to investigate it. The sense of smell is one on which cats rely heavily. You may observe your cat sniffing various things around the home, including you, when she has gotten a whiff of a new odor. If the odor is pleasing, your cat may rub her head or body against it or even lick the spot. If she withdraws from the odor and appears to stare with gaping mouth for a few seconds, it is because she has encountered an unpleasant odor with the olfactory organs inside her mouth.

Her facial expressions— ear position, eye movement and facial muscle movement— provide clues to the workings of your cat's mind.

TAIL MOVEMENTS

Cats use their tails to communicate, just as they use the rest of their bodies. A cat who is relaxed and contented will hold her tail at an angle slightly higher than parallel with her body as she walks. A cat who is agitated or excited will flick her tail back and forth. A cat who is unhappy or experiencing stress or depression may appear to drag her tail behind her. A cat who is happy or being petted will raise her tail to a relaxed upward position.

The "up tail" position can be observed between two cats who have bonded or are part of the same social group. The sudden, upward flick of the tail as they pass each other is a form of acceptance or friendly greeting.

In social hierarchies, a cat will present her posterior region to a more dominant cat. A raised tail enables the dominant cat to smell the anal area of a subordinate. Mutual sniffing of anterior regions is a manner in which cats gain acceptance with other cats in the group. Because you are the dominant member of the household, your cat may appear to stick her rear end in your face at various times. Although this may seem unpleasant, it is really a form of flattery.

A cat's tail is a very expressive feature.

VOCALIZATIONS

Cats communicate vocally as well as through body language. Some cats are more vocal than others, but as a general rule, vocal communication occurs when a cat wants to say something to his owner or to another cat, such as when two males square off for the affections of a female in heat, and will increase when you speak to him. The Siamese, for example, is known to be a "talker." Its voice is loud and forceful. Other cats may trill, burble, chirp or let out with the classic "meow." Some may combine sounds into distinctive phrases that will come to mean

121

something to you as you get to know your cat more intimately. In every case, the sounds your cat makes are intended to tell you something or request something from you. Translating your feline's unique "cat talk" is one of the ongoing adventures of living with a feline.

The most common sound among cats and the one most pleasing to their owners is the purr. Cats purr as a form a communication. A mother will purr to her kittens to guide them to milk and as a form of reassurance. Adult cats will purr to other cats, to their owners and to themselves for countless reasons or

Cats purr when they are content and comfortable.

for no reason at all. They purr when they are contented, when they are nervous (for example, when visiting the vet), and also when they are injured or dying. Some cats seem to purr continuously, while others reserve their purrs for special occasions. Some cats may stop purring if circumstances are not to their liking. Although two theories exist— the movement of air over the vocal cords or the flow of blood through the vena cava vein—no one is really sure how a cat purrs. Whatever the reason, the soothing and hypnotic sound is unique to cats.

Another sound that is uniquely feline is that of two males vying for a female. Their vocalizations can range from a low growl or a moderately pitched cry to a high-pitched scream, depending on the level of stress each is experiencing or how intensely they are trying to scare off the other. When one hears two toms fighting, especially at night, their cries have a haunting, eerie quality and can often be mistaken for a baby crying.

SOCIAL BEHAVIOR

When kittens want to nurse, they knead their claws against their mothers' stomachs to stimulate the flow of milk. Cats continue this behavior as adults. A human owner will replace a cat's feline mother in many ways, and your cat will knead you in the same way she kneaded her mother, particularly when she is relaxed and preparing to sleep.

Cats are territorial in nature and like a space, whether inside or outside the home, that is theirs. Cats rub against their surroundings to mark their territories. They also rub against things because the sensation is pleasing to them and is a form of self-grooming, smoothing the hair in the direction it grows. Your cat will rub against you for various reasons—as an expression of positive feelings for you, as a way to let you know she wants something (like dinner), as an expression of pure pleasure such as when she is being petted or as a way of marking you as part of her territory. Regardless of the reason, being rubbed by your cat is a form of affection and should be returned with affection from you.

When Problems Arise

What is normal behavior for cats living outdoors—clawing, jumping up on things, territorial marking—can become a problem when the cat engages in these behaviors indoors. Even the most conscientious cat owner may find that his or her cat develops an occasional behavior problem that must be corrected. According to the American Animal Hospital Association, more cats and dogs are euthanized each year because of behavior problems than for any medical reason. Working with your cat to solve a behavior problem will make your cat a better pet.

The first and foremost rule when trying to solve a behavior problem is no physical punishment. Hitting or swatting your cat does nothing to correct the problem and only creates mistrust. Some cat owners spritz their cats with a squirt gun when the cat does something the owner does not like, such as jumping on the kitchen counter. But in order for this method to be successful, you must catch your cat in the act, which usually requires that you be armed with your squirt gun every moment you are in the house. Also, a cat soon learns simply to avoid her owner and that when the owner is away, she can do pretty much as she pleases.

Understanding what your cat is telling you by her actions will help you alter her inappropriate behavior. Solving behavior problems involves a two-pronged attack. The first is working with your cat to modify her behavior; and the second is, if necessary, modifying your environment to create one that is more acceptable from a feline perspective, yet livable for you.

ELIMINATION PROBLEMS

One of the most common problems, especially with indoor cats, is inappropriate elimination—urinating or defecating out of the litter box. Although urinating out of the box is by far more common, defecating outside the litter box occurs occasionally. If your cat engages in either of these behaviors, have her checked by a veterinarian first to make certain that her behavior is not caused by a medical reason.

Do not rub your cat's nose in her wastes. It will only make your cat fear you and will not solve the problem. Elimination problems can be due to a variety of reasons, most of which center around the litter box itself. Some can be a result of stress or changes in the home environment. For those situations, removing the source of the stress or helping the cat adjust to change will solve the problem.

If your cat eliminates just outside of or near her box, it could be due to three major factors: The litter is not kept clean, the box is not appealing for some reason, or the litter is unacceptable to your cat. The first condition is easily corrected. The most common cause of a cat refusing to use her litter box is that the box is dirty. Removal of urine and feces at least once a day is necessary to keep the box clean and appealing to your cat. To help you in that task, purchase a large litter scoop or line the box with plastic liners.

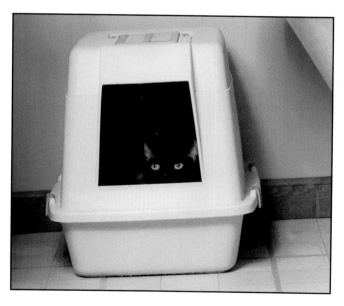

If your cat is experiencing elimination problems, make sure the kind of litterbox and its placement in your home are comfortable for your cat.

Some cats may object to the type of litter box: It's too small, it's covered, or it's made of a material that a cat does not like. Experimenting with different types of litter boxes or non-traditional boxes such as dish pans or large plastic storage bins may solve the problem. In addition, many cats prefer to use one litter box to urinate and another to defecate, so buying two boxes, perhaps even placing them in two separate locations, may be all that it takes to convince your cat to potty where she's supposed to.

The type of litter material or brand of litter may affect your cat's potty habits as well. Experiment with types of clay, sand, wood chips or other organic materials to find a litter your cat likes. Sometimes the solution can be as simple as going from a scented to unscented litter. Cats occasionally show a preference for different substrates in which to bury their wastes, such as shredded newspaper or carpet. Filling the litter box with those materials may help your cat get used to her box, at least long enough to gradually convert it to a more easily maintained substance. Some cats prefer not to stand in litter, so putting litter at just one end of the box will provide your cat with both a clean place to stand and a place to bury her deposits.

If your cat eliminates in a location in your home distant from the box, other factors may be playing a part in her behavior. The location of the box may discourage your cat from wanting to use it. If your cat must go past Rover's bed to get to her litter box or walk across a wet basement floor, the trip may not be worth the effort. Try moving the box to a location that is more comfortable for your cat.

If your cat is eliminating in one or two spots continuously, place her litter box on that spot and gradually move the box back to a good location. Or change the function of that spot by placing the food bowls there. Once the odor of a previous elimination permeates a particular spot, a cat may choose it again and again. Use an odor-removing cleaning product to discourage your cat from returning to the same place.

AGGRESSION

The most common form of aggression cats exhibit is "play biting." Cats learn this form of behavior as kittens when they play with littermates, and they may transfer it to their human owners. Your cat may attack your feet as they move under the covers at night or as you step out of the shower. A nip on the hand as you are petting your cat may say, "Ok, I've had enough" or a swat at your ankles as you walk by may say, "Hey, I want some attention." This form of aggression is not serious and usually results in no harm to the owner. If it is unappreciated, tell your cat "no" in a loud firm voice when it happens. Accompanying the command by snapping the fingers or clapping your hands will distract your cat from the activity you want to stop. Repetition will help train her.

Playing with your cat and providing exercise will help dispel her playful aggression. Interactive cat toys or games of retrieval that force your cat to run, jump and chase will work off some of that excess energy that is building up and making her attack you instead of a toy.

Occasionally, a cat may become seriously aggressive. Her attacks may be directed toward other animals, people in general or those of a particular sex or age, such as young children. In most cases the aggression is motivated by the cat's effort to defend herself from what she perceives as a danger. When she feels threatened, she may combine her attacks with spitting, hissing and growling. Serious aggression may result in scratches, breaking the skin and subsequent bleeding or even puncture wounds. A knowledge of a cat's past history may go a long way in explaining her aggressive tendencies. Being attacked by another animal, physically punished or abused by a former owner or mistreated or mishandled by a child may have caused her to generalize her fear, and consequently, the cat reacts aggressively to stimuli in her current environment that

SPRAYING

Inappropriate urination and spraying are often mistakenly thought to be the same thing. Urination is a physiological function, and your cat does it simply to eliminate wastes. A cat sprays, however, as a behavioral function, and does it to mark territory.

Spraying can be distinguished from urination by the body position a cat assumes when performing each function. Cats squat to urinate on a horizontal surface such as the litter box. Cats stand to spray, which is squirting urine on a vertical surface such as a wall. Both male and female cats spray, but it is far more common among males. The presence of an intact cat, even outside the home, may cause a cat inside the home to begin spraying behavior. Neutering or spaying your cat is the most effective way to solve the problem of spraying before it starts.

appear similar to those in her past—that is, a man, a woman, a dog or a child.

Solving this kind of aggression will take time and patience but will be well worth the effort. If your cat exhibits defensive aggression, leave her alone and allow her to calm down. Do not try to pet her or pick her up. Because she feels threatened, this will only make the situation worse. If your cat is aggressive toward another animal, remove the animal from her environment. Reintroduce them slowly and for small amounts of time under your supervision until they become accustomed to each other.

If the aggression is directed toward a specific person, make sure the person does not engage in any movement that further frightens your cat. One good way to get your cat on friendly terms with the person she appears not to like is to allow him or her to feed your cat. Feeding will help "break the ice" between a defensively aggressive cat and the object of her aggression. If necessary, isolate your cat from the object of her aggression and gradually reintroduce her under controlled conditions.

BUSPIRONE

Buspirone is a human antipsychotic drug that is being used to help solve aggressive behavior in cats. Buspirone does not have the long-term side effects that other drugs may have, such as valium. Buspirone has also been effective in stopping territorial spraying.

Drug therapy should be a last resort in solving behavior problems. If you have been unable to solve your cat's aggression, discuss the possibility of using Buspirone or other therapies with your veterinarian.

FEAR OF LOUD NOISES

Many cats exhibit a fear of loud noises. Thunder, fireworks, backfiring cars, vacuum cleaners, stereos, even the sound of an object dropping in the home can spook a cat and send her scurrying for cover. Keeping an environment free of as much sudden, loud noise as possible will go a long way in helping your cat overcome her fear, but a cat owner can't control the noises that occur outside of the home, least of all those caused by the weather.

The purpose of addressing noise phobias is not to condition your cat to loud noises, but to make her as comfortable as possible when they occur and to build up her trust in both you as caregiver and her home as a safe place to be. Over time, your cat will gradually lose some of her fear and become accustomed to sounds that occur regularly inside and outside the home, such as that of a vacuum cleaner or lawnmower.

If your cat wants to hide and deal with her fear the best way she knows how, let her. There is no rule that says a cat must be able to tolerate loud sounds. If your cat wants to hide during thunderstorms or municipal holiday fireworks, provide her with a place that is as far away from windows and the source of the noise as possible. Play some soft music on the radio to help muffle the sounds and make your cat relax.

If your cat jumps onto table tops before dinner, try feeding her before you prepare your own meal.

UNDESIRABLE JUMPING

Jumping onto furniture for a snooze is one of the pastimes that will occupy your cat's day. Because cats like to jump to seek comfort or as a form of exercise, your cat may jump onto things that you would prefer to keep her off of, such as the dining room table and the kitchen countertops.

Cats typically jump onto countertops and tables to look for food. Feeding your cat before you begin preparing your meal will eliminate her hunger and help discourage her from looking for additional sensual gratification in your kitchen. Cats typically opt for a personal grooming session and a nap after breakfast and dinner, so chances are that your cat will leave your kitchen counters and dining table alone after she has eaten.

If your cat still insists on being involved in your meal activities, confine her to another room of the house during those times or train her to jump on a climbing tree as a substitute. (See Chapter 11 for tips on how to train a cat to stay down from undesirable surfaces.)

Booby Traps

Some behaviorists and cat experts recommend setting up booby traps in those places around your home that you don't want your cat to go. Electric mats that emit a shock to discourage a cat from stepping on certain spots, stacks of aluminum cans that make noise when they fall, upside-down mouse traps that snap shut when a cat comes into contact with them—all these techniques have been recommended as methods of modifying a cat's undesirable behavior.

These methods, however, have some real drawbacks. First, devices that require electricity to perform their intended function are a danger to any animal that makes as much use of her claws as a cat does. When a cat jumps on an electric mat, she completes the electrical circuit, and the mat gives her a small shock. Any person who touches the mat also gets an electric shock. Electric mats also require that they remain plugged into an outlet to work. If the device is near water, such as on the kitchen counter, it could pose a hazard from more severe electric shock. The presence of an electric mat or other types of booby traps on a kitchen counter, for example, prevents that area from being of use to you as the cat owner.

Booby-trapping with objects that make noise also frightens a cat when she comes into contact with them. The goal of any training method should be to teach a cat what to do and what not to do through positive learning experiences rather than negative ones. In households where there are children, noisy booby traps could be just as frightening to a child who accidentally comes into contact with them. As a cat owner, you will be better off spending your time using positive techniques that build a bond of trust between the two of you rather than using methods that try to modify behavior by instilling fear.

Kitty Psychiatrists

If your cat has a behavior problem that you have been unable to solve, consulting a pet therapist or certified animal behaviorist may help. Pet therapists are usually self-trained and have extensive experience dealing with pets and their problems. A certified animal behaviorist has obtained at least a master's degree in animal behavior and has been certified by the Animal Behavior Society.

A pet therapist or behaviorist will consult with you and observe your cat in her home environment. He or she will formulate an extensive history of your cat and her behavior before recommending a corrective program. When hiring a behavior consultant, ask for references of other cats he or she has helped. Like your veterinarian, this person should also be somebody with whom you feel comfortable. Make sure that any fees are understood and discussed up front.

PET CONSULTANT TO THE STARS

For more than twenty-five years, internationally known pet and animal expert Warren Eckstein has been teaching both pets and their people how to live happily together through his unique "Hugs and Kisses" approach to animal behavior, care and training.

Eckstein has worked with more than 40,000 pets, including those of David Letterman, Cheryl Tiegs, Lily Tomlin, Geraldine Ferraro, Al Pacino, Rodney Dangerfield and Roy Scheider. He has been regularly featured on *Live! With Regis and Kathie Lee* and *Today in New York*, and as the creature keeper on the Disney Channel's *New Mickey Mouse Club.*

Eckstein is a "hands-on" animal expert and has treated all kinds of animals. His books *How to Get Your Cat to Do What You Want*, *The Illustrated Cat's Life* and *Pet Aerobics* help cat owners have happier, healthier and better-behaved pets.

Behavior consulting is still a new field, and there are relatively few certified behaviorists across the country. To find a pet therapist, consult your local telephone directory, your veterinarian or a local animal shelter. Shelters in large urban areas often have a behaviorist on staff or operate a behavior hotline.

To find a certified animal behaviorist, contact the Animal Behavior Society (see Chapter 14, "Resources").

chapter 11

Training
Your
Cat

Every year, domestic felines appear in movies, on television shows and in commercials. They come, stay, run, walk and do whatever else a script may demand. Like their king-sized counterparts in circuses—lions, tigers, jaguars and other large roaring cats of the family Panthera who have been trained to perform—domestic cats are regularly trained by professional animal trainers to perform stunts, tricks and a plethora of things that most cat owners would like their cats to do. In spite of these success

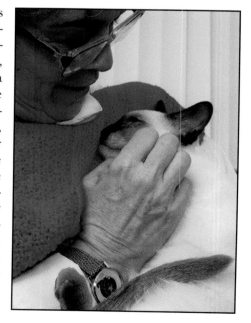

stories, many people still don't believe that cats can be trained.

If you would like to train your cat or simply modify his behavior to correct inappropriate actions, you can use the same techniques professional animal trainers use to help your cat learn simple commands and behave in ways that are more suitable to life with humans.

Reward your cat with a treat when he performs the correct behavior.

One of the keys to training your cat is communication. Obviously, humans and animals do not speak the same language. In order to communicate your wishes to your cat, you must speak in simple terms your cat can understand. The language of "yes" and

"no," when used to indicate appropriate and inappropriate behavior, will help your cat learn what he is to do and not to do. Commands that you want your cat to learn, such as "come here," "sit" or "stay" should remain simple one- or two-word phrases.

As the owner of a cat who never intends to appear in movies or television, you may question the usefulness of training your cat to sit, stay or respond to other verbal commands. But consider the number of times you leave your home through the front door and do not want your cat to follow you. A cat who knows how to sit or stay is less likely to dart outside under his owner's feet when he hears his owner give the command. A cat who understands simple commands such as "down" or "get down" and is rewarded for those behaviors will get out or off of places he should not be in when his owner tells him to.

A second key to training your cat is consistency. Any commands or behaviors you are trying to teach your cat must be applied consistently, using the same simple terminology. It does you and your cat no good to apply a command for a behavior one time and not the next, or to use one word as the command one time and another the next. Inconsistency only confuses your cat and does not achieve the result you desire—a well-behaved, well-trained animal.

And third, any training you undertake with your cat should be based on a reward system, not on punishment or other negative methods of behavior modification. Cats do not accept reprimands well, and it is unfair to punish a cat for behaving inappropriately if you have not taken the time to train him. From the cat's point of view, the behavior he displays is completely natural. It is only from the owner's point of view that it is inappropriate.

When teaching your cat the following commands, have treats ready as a reward. Make the treats something special to your cat that may not be a part of his normal diet, such as bits of tuna or boiled chicken, and offer the food rewards in small quantities.

"Come"

When you must take your cat to the vet, wouldn't it be less stressful for you and your cat if your cat came when you called his name rather than scurrying under the bed the moment he sees the carrier? This is just one instance of many in which knowing your cat will come when called would be not only useful but potentially lifesaving.

Coming when called is probably one of the easiest commands to teach a cat. Your cat is already positively motivated to come to you because he knows that he will receive attention, affection and love. At mealtimes, he knows that he will receive food.

Using your cat's natural inclination to come for his meals is a good way to begin training him to come when called. Just before your cat's next meal, call "Fluffy, come here!" Some cat owners have successfully used hand signals to motion their cats to come when giving the command. Some professional trainers also use a cricket or other device to make a clicking sound when they give a command and when they offer the food reward. You may also tap a bowl lightly with a spoon instead of the clicker. If you want to train by using a noise-making device, the clicker is easier to carry when you are teaching other commands. When your cat comes, make the clicking noise and praise him as you repeat the command and give him the food reward.

Repeat the process until your cat comes when he hears his name. Keep this and other training sessions short—about ten or fifteen minutes at a time. Always give your cat lots of praise and his food reward when he behaves correctly.

"Stay"

Knowing the "stay" command will help keep your cat from getting into things he is not supposed to and may keep him from going out the door when he shouldn't. To train your cat to stay, begin working with him in a quiet room, free of distractions. As your cat comes toward you, extend your arm and put your hand out as if you

---

PROFESSIONAL ANIMAL TRAINER, SCOTT HART

Scott Hart is one of the foremost animal trainers in the entertainment industry. His cats retrieve, stand on their hind legs, sit, lie down, roll over, stop on a mark, touch a prop, wave, box and respond to many other commands. For more than twenty years, he has trained some of the most famous feline stars. His four-member Friskies Cat Team—including two American Shorthairs named Nitro Mouse and Woody, a British Shorthair named Monty and a Somali named Liberty—appears in movies and on stage and travels across the United States to promote and demonstrate cat training.

Hart began his career working with the lion stars for the series *Born Free* under the tutelage of wild animal trainer Hubert Wells. After achieving success with wild animals, Hart decided to broaden his scope to include domestic animals, such as birds, dogs and cats.

His movie credits include *The Shawshank Redemption, True Lies,* Stephen King's *Pet Cemetery, Raising Arizona, Beaches, Darkman* and *Ferris Bueller's Day Off,* and the television movie *Strays,* among others.

were a policeman directing traffic. Give the command, "stay." When your cat stops, praise him and give him a small treat. Continue the process, moving farther back from your cat when you put out your hand and say, "stay." If your cat decides to do something else instead of enduring the lesson, bring him back to the starting point and begin again. Each time your cat reacts appropriately, give him the food reward and lots of praise.

To teach your cat to stay, extend your hand in a stop gesture.

Once you've trained your cat to stay, you don't want him sitting in the same position forever. Once he knows the "stay" command, you must give another command to let him know that it is alright to go. Getting up from the floor and using the other command your cat knows, "come," is a good way to release your cat from his stay position.

Walking on a Harness

Your cat will love some time outdoors, especially if you've opted to make your cat an indoor-only pet for health and safety reasons. One of the safest ways to allow your cat outside is to take him for a walk on a harness.

To begin, make sure the harness fits properly. A harness should be tight enough around the cat's middle but allow enough room for you to slip two fingers between the harness and his body. Accustom your cat to the harness while indoors. Associate the experience with something positive, like a meal.

Allow your cat to wear the harness indoors for about two weeks. When your cat is comfortable wearing it, attach a leash. Do not take your cat outside yet. Hold a piece of food treat in front of your cat close enough for him smell it. Give the command, "Tigger, heel" and move forward slowly. When your cat takes a step forward, say "heel" again and give him the food immediately along with lots of praise.

Repeat the process until your cat learns the word "heel." Once you feel your cat knows the command and is comfortable walking on a leash, take him outside. Begin walking outside around the yard or close to home. With practice, you can walk your cat on a leash for longer distances.

As a word of caution, however, do not leave your cat on a leash unattended outside. Because the cat is leashed, he is powerless to escape any threats from stray cats, dogs or other animals who may come by. Always accompany your cat while he is on harness.

chapter 12

Having Fun

with Your

Cat

Living with a cat will provide you with hours of enjoyment and the opportunity to spend many special moments with your feline companion. But being a cat owner will also propel you into a world of cat-related activities in which you can participate with other cat lovers and your own cat. Here are a few suggestions for ways to spend your spare time. Turn to Chapters 13 and 14 for additional information about the organizations mentioned.

Cat Shows

One of the most enjoyable activities associated with having a cat is becoming involved with the cat fancy. Regardless of whether you want to enter your special cat in a show or just attend one for fun, cat shows offer owners an opportunity to see some of the best cats in each of the many breeds, meet other cat fanciers and shop for cat products from the many vendors who exhibit at each show.

Before you decide to enter your cat in a show, do some homework. Visit some cat shows and look at the cats who are entered. Find out beforehand what judges look for in each breed category, and observe the judging. Contact the registry that interests you to obtain a list of its rules and breed standards.

If you plan to enter a cat show, familiarize yourself beforehand with the qualities the judges are looking for.

If you have a show-quality purebred cat, you can compete in one of the four pedigreed categories. Cats between the ages of four and eight months compete with other kittens of the same breed, sex and color for first-, second- and third-place ribbons in the Kitten category. Additional ribbons are awarded for color class. Altered pedigreed cats more than eight months of age compete in the Premiership category and are judged by the same standards as intact cats. Unaltered pedigreed cats compete in the Championship category.

If your cat is a pet-quality purebred or a random breed, you may want to enter her in the Happy Household Pet division. Cats entered into the HHP category must be altered if more than eight months of age, have all of their adult attributes and not be declawed. Although the HHP category does not offer championships, you will share in the fun and excitement of competition and have the opportunity to win ribbons for your cat. HHPs are judged on their uniqueness, pleasing appearance, unusual markings and personalities.

Once you decide to enter a cat show, check the dates of upcoming ones in the major cat magazines (see Chapter 13, "Additional Reading"). Each magazine has a calendar section that lists upcoming shows and the name, address and telephone number of the entry clerk to contact. Once you decide which show you want to enter, request a show flyer and entry form. Complete the form and send it with the entry fee before the deadline.

If showing your cat is a goal, accustom her to being handled before the show. Examine her as a judge would, and offer a treat or some playtime following each session. When in the ring, a judge will handle a cat in certain ways to evaluate certain characteristics. This involves checking her stance, lifting her up and examining her ears, face, hair and tail.

When not being judged, your cat will stay in an assigned cage in the benching area. Cat shows are long, and the time in a cage can be stressful for some cats. If you observe your cat being stressed in a competition environment, it is best not to show her.

In all categories, including household pet, a cat must be in top condition, alert, healthy, well-groomed and easy to handle. Bathe and brush your cat and clip her nails. Have your cat tested to make sure she is FeLV-negative. Make sure her vaccinations are current. At a show, you do not want to pass along any diseases to other cats, and you do not want your cat to be at risk.

While at the show hall, as an exhibitor or visitor, observe show-hall etiquette. Refrain from petting cats without permission to avoid passing along any harmful microorganisms. Many of the cats entered into a show are unaltered and may react to the smell of another cat on your hands.

Cat Clubs

Another way to have fun with your cat and meet other cat lovers is to join a special-interest club. The Cat Collector's Club is a national organization whose members enjoy reading about and collecting cat-related items. Members collect any and all objects related to domestic or wild cats, or specialize in types of collectibles such as cat plates, figurines, postcards, prints, antique cats, miniatures or items relating to a specific breed.

A show cat should be in top condition: alert, healthy and well-groomed.

Members of Cat Collectors receive a bimonthly newsletter containing illustrated articles about antique as well as new cat collectibles, book reviews and shopping tips. Members also have the opportunity to meet other collectors at regularly held conventions.

If you would like to get together with people in your geographic location, why not start your own cat club? Members could meet regularly, tell stories about their cats and share cat-care and housekeeping tips. At meetings, participants can show and discuss cat-care videos and books obtained from a local library. Invite local cat experts or shelter personnel to give a talk. Your club activities are limited only by your imagination.

If you would like your pet cat to compete for rosettes and earn titles just like the purebreds, the Happy Household Pet Cat Club offers its members the opportunity to participate in the fun and excitement of cat shows. Formed in 1968 in Sacramento, California, HHPCC has more than seven hundred members in the United States and Canada. Purebred cat registries who have HHP categories obtain winning rosettes from the Happy Household Pet Cat Club for upcoming shows. Winning cats are scored, and yearly awards go out to the Top Cats and Kittens. Members receive a newsletter with information of interest to all cat lovers—cat and animal welfare, cat show reports, cat poems, cat pictures, anecdotes, book reviews and health articles.

Pets on the Net

If you have a personal computer and a modem, you may want to obtain access to the Internet. The Inter-net is a connection of more than three million computers all over the world that enables subscribers to access a vast array of information resources. You will be able to participate in discussion groups with other cat lovers, share stories and anecdotes about cats, ask advice and even pose questions to animal behaviorists, veterinarians and others in related fields.

Discussion groups on "the Net" are called listserves. Some of the cat and animal-related listserves are listed below. To obtain information about how to subscribe to these once you have access to the Internet, turn to Chapter 14, "Resources."

VETMED-L is a discussion group for pet and farm animal owners, veterinary students and veterinarians. It is an active list, generating more than fifty messages per day.

FANCIERS' NET is a specialized list focused on cat breeding, exhibiting and related topics. It, too, is an active list often generating more than eighty postings per day.

FELINE-L is a discussion list for anyone interested in cats. Its related activity, FUR (Feline Underground Railroad), engages in rescuing and placing adoptable cats.

The newsgroup rec.pets.cats is a bulletin board for anyone interested in talking about felines. No subscription is necessary.

Through pet-assisted therapy, your cat can offer affection and comfort to those who cannot keep their own pets.

There are many ways to obtain Internet access. Some large computer network providers such as Compuserve, America Online and Prodigy offer Internet access. Another way to obtain it is from a local provider such as a telephone or cable television company. For local providers in your geographic area, contact your local phone and cable companies or library.

Pet-Assisted Therapy

The benefits of having a pet are innumerable. Documented cases have shown mental patients who have not spoken or moved on their own for years responding to stroking a cat and hearing her purr. Caring for animals gives the elderly a renewed sense of self-worth and interest in what is occurring around them.

Unfortunately, some of the people who might benefit most from having a pet are unable to do so because they have disabilities or live in nursing homes or institutions. To help disadvantaged individuals experience the joys of being around a pet, many shelters and animal organizations sponsor pet-assisted therapy programs.

Volunteers in pet therapy programs visit nursing homes and institutions with affectionate, easy-going animals. The volunteers spend time with the residents, allowing them to hold and pet the visiting animals. Organizers of pet therapy programs train volunteers and usually use animals who are able to remain unstressed around strangers and in new environments.

*Pets contribute
to both our
physical and
mental
well-being.*

If you would like to take part in a pet therapy program, contact a local shelter to find out whether any are already in operation. If you would like to start your own pet therapy program, contact the Delta Society, which can provide information about training to become a pet therapy volunteer. The Delta Society offers training around the country for those wishing to help others through pet-assisted therapy.

Helping Cats in Need

One of the most gratifying activities you can engage in is helping cats who are less fortunate than the one you have adopted. Millions of cats die every year in shelters across the country because there are not enough homes for them.

If you would like to help cats in need, volunteer your time to a local animal organization or shelter. Many agencies exist across the country, with a variety of goals. Some are low-cost spay/neuter organizations, some rescue cats at large, and some are educational agencies. Others operate shelters, feline foster parent or adoption programs. Most animal organizations need volunteers to help in fund-raising, publish newsletters, develop educational activities, clean cages and socialize animals.

If you have time to offer, call a local animal organization and ask what you can do to help. By helping cats in your hometown, you will be helping cats everywhere.

part four

Beyond the Basics

chapter 13

Additional Reading

Books

The following books will provide you with additional information about your cat and how to care for him. Some of the books listed may no longer be in print, so contact you local library for a copy.

GENERAL

Fox, Dr. Michael W. *Supercat: Raising the Perfect Feline Companion*. New York: Howell Book House, 1990.

Hammond, Sean and Carolyn Usrey. *How to Raise a Sane and Healthy Cat*. New York: Howell Book House, 1994.

Jankowski, Connie. *Adopting Cats and Kittens: A Care and Training Guide*. New York: Howell Book House, 1993.

Levy, Juliette de Bairacli. *Cats Naturally*. London: Faber and Faber, 1991.

Nemec, Gale B. *Living with Cats*. New York: William Morrow, 1993.

Pyles, Mary. *Everyday Cat: The Complete Guide to Understanding and Enjoying Your Pet Cat*. New York: Howell Book House, 1991.

Taylor, David. *You and Your Cat*. New York: Alfred A. Knopf, 1990.

BEHAVIOR AND TRAINING

Caras, Roger. *A Cat Is Watching: A Look at the Way Cats See Us*. New York: Simon & Schuster, 1990.

Eckstein, Warren and Fay Eckstein. *How to Get Your Cat to Do What You Want*. Villard Books, 1990.

Fogle, Bruce. *Know Your Cat: An Owner's Guide to Cat Behavior.* New York: Dorling Kindersley, 1991.

Fogle, Bruce. *101 Questions Your Cat Would Ask Its Vet (If Your Cat Could Talk)*. Carroll and Graf Publishers, Inc., 1993.

Humphries, Jim, DVM. *Dr. Jim's Animal Clinic for Cats*. New York: Howell Book House, 1994.

Kunkel, Paul. *How to Toilet Train Your Cat: 21 Days to a Litter-Free Cat*. New York: Workman's, 1991.

Morris, Desmond. *Catlore*. New York: Crown, 1987.

Siegal, Mordecai. *Understanding the Cat You Love*. New York: Berkeley Books, 1994.

Smith, Carin A. *One Hundred Training Tips for Your Cat*. New York: Dell Publishing Company, 1994.

Thomas, Elizabeth Marshall. *Tribe of the Tiger: Cats and Their Culture*. New York: Simon & Schuster, 1994.

Wilbourn, Carole. *Cat Talk: What Your Cat is Trying to Tell You*. New York: Publisher's Choice, 1991.

HEALTH AND NUTRITION

Bell, Charles T. P. *First Aid and Health Care for Cats*. Berkeley Books, 1991.

Frazier, Anita. *The New Natural Cat: A Complete Guide for Finicky Owners*. New York: Plume Books, 1990.

Hawcroft, Tim. *First Aid for Cats: The Essential Quick-Reference Guide*. New York: Howell Book House, 1994.

Lawson, Tony. *The Cat Lover's Cookbook: Recipes*. New York: Random House, 1994.

McGinnis, Terri. *The Well Cat Book: The Classic Comprehensive Handbook of Cat Care*. New York: Random House, 1993.

Pinney, Chris S. *Guide to Home Pet Grooming: Everything about Your Pet's Skin and Coat, Including Nutrition, Basic and Advanced Grooming, and the Latest Information on*

Parasites, Allergies and Other Common Skin and Hair Coat Disorders. New York: Barron's, 1990.

Pitcairn, Richard H. *Dr. Pitcairn's Complete Guide to Natural Health for Dogs and Cats.* Emmaus, Pa.: Rodale Press, 1995.

Siegal, Mordecai, ed. *The Cornell Book of Cats: A Comprehensive Medical Reference for Every Cat and Kitten.* New York: Villard Books, 1989.

Wolff, H. G., DVM. *Your Healthy Cat: Homeopathic Medicines for Common Feline Ailments.* Berkeley: North Atlantic Books, 1991.

CAT BREEDS AND SHOWING

Gebhardt, Richard H. *The Complete Cat Book.* New York: Howell Book House, 1991.

Maggitti, Phil, et al. *Owning the Right Cat.* Blacksburg, VA: Tetra Press, 1993.

McGonagle, John J. and Carolyn M. Vella. *In the Spotlight: A Guide to Showing Pedigreed and Household Pet Cats.* New York: Howell Publishing, 1990.

YOUR CAT

Phoebe Phillips Editions, *Cat Calls: Cat Names Through the Ages.* New York: E. P. Dutton, 1988.

MISCELLANEOUS

Barrie, Anmarie, Esq. *Cats and the Law.* New Jersey: T.F.H. Publications, 1990.

de Caro, Frank. *The Folktale Cat.* Little Rock: August House Publishers, 1992.

Ney, George. *Cat Condominiums and Other Feline Furniture.* New York: E. P. Dutton, 1989.

Cat Magazines

Reading cat-related magazines will help keep you up-to-date on the latest cat-care information. You can write to these addresses for subscription information or purchase a copy of the magazine at your local newsstand and use one of the subscription cards inside.

Cat Fancy
Subscriptions
P.O. Box 52864
Boulder, CO 80322-2864
303/666-8504

CATS Magazine
Subscription Department
P.O. Box 40240
Palm Coast, FL 32142-0240
904/445-2828

I Love Cats
I Love Cats Publishing Company, Inc.
P.O. Box 7013
Red Oak, IA 51591-0013

Tiger Tribe
1407 East College Street
Iowa City, IA 52245-4410
319/351-6698

Books and Videos for Your Cat

Schwartz, Alvin. *Stories to Tell a Cat.* New York: Harper Collins, 1992.

Pet Avision, Inc., *Video Catnip: Entertainment for Cats.* Box 222, Lyndon Center, VT 05850.

Videos for You

Fox, Michael W. *Cat Care: A Video Guide to Successful Cat Care.* New York: Maier Group Communications, 1987.

Groomers Guide to the Cat

Kittens to Cats

chapter 14

Resources

Cat Registries

There are six U.S. purebred cat registries. If you would like to purchase a purebred cat or obtain information about a registry's standards, rules and regulations or exhibiting procedures, contact them at the addresses listed below.

American Association of Cat Enthusiasts
P.O. Box 213
Pine Brook, NJ 07058

American Cat Association
8101 Katherine Avenue
Panorama City, CA 91402

American Cat Fanciers' Association
P.O. Box 203
Pt. Lookout, MO 65726

Cat Fanciers' Association
P.O. Box 1005
Manasquan, NJ 08736-0805

Cat Fanciers' Federation
9509 Montgomery Road
Cincinnati, OH 45242

The International Cat Association (TICA)
P.O. Box 2684
Harlingen, TX 78551

Cat Clubs

For more information about joining these cat clubs,
send a self-addressed, stamped envelope to the
addresses below.

Calico Cat Registry International
P.O. Box 944
Morongo Valley, CA 92256

Cat Collectors
33161 Wendy Drive
Sterling Heights, MI 48310

Happy Household Pet Cat Club
c/o Florine Jones
8862 Sharkey Avenue
Elk Grove, CA 95624

Socks the Cat Fan Club
Presidential Socks Partnership, Inc.
611 S. Ivy Street
Arlington, VA 22204

Mail-Order Catalogs

Many companies sell cat products through the mail.
The companies listed below will send their product
catalogs free of charge.

Care-A-Lot Pet Supply Warehouse
1617 Diamond Springs Road
Virginia Beach, VA 23455
804/460-9771 (in Virginia)
800/343-7680

Cats, Cats and More Cats
P.O. Box 270
Route 17M
Monroe, NY 10950

Cherrybrook
Route 57, Box 15
Broadway, NJ 08808
800/524-0820

Discount Master Animal Care Catalog
Division of Humboldt Industries, Inc.
Lake Road, P.O. Box 3333
Mountaintop, PA 18707-0330
800/346-0749

Doctors Foster and Smith
2253 Air Park Road
P.O. Box 100
Rhinelander, WI 54501-0100
800/826-7206

Dr. A. C. Daniels
109 Worcester Road
Webster, MA 01570
800/547-3760

Felix
3623 Fremont Ave., N.
Seattle, WA 98103

Hep Cat
P.O. Box 40223
Nashville, TN 37204

New England Serum Company
Groomer/Kennel Products Division
P.O. Box 128
Topsfield, MA 01983

Pedigrees: The Pet Catalog
1989 Transit Way, Box 905
Brockport, NY 14420-0905
800/548-4786

Pet Warehouse
Dept. C28D
P.O. Box 310
Xenia, OH 45385
800/443-1160

Summit Pet Products
400 Quaint Acres Drive
Silver Spring, MD 10904
800/882-9410

UPCO
P.O. Box 969
St. Joseph, MO 64502
800/444-8651

Cat/Animal Organizations

These organizations will refer you to services in your geographic area. When writing to these organizations, enclose a self-addressed, stamped envelope for a response.

American Holistic Veterinary Medical Association
2214 Old Emmorton Road
Bel Air, MD 21015

Animal Behavior Society
c/o Dr. Suzanne Hetts
Animal Behavior Associates
4994 S. Independence Way
Littleton, CO 80123-1906

Delta Society
Pet Partners Program
P.O. Box 1080
Renton, WA 98057-9906

International Veterinary Acupuncture Society
2140 Conestoga Road
Chester Springs, PA 19425

National Association of Pet Sitters
Pet Sitters International Referral Hotline
800/268-SITS (7487)

Internet Providers

The following companies offer access to the Internet as part of their subscriptions. Write or call for more information.

America On-Line
8619 Westwood Center Drive
Vienna, VA 22182-2285
800/827-3338

CompuServe
P.O. Box 20212
Columbus, OH 43220
800/609-1674

Prodigy Services Company
22 North Plains Industrial Highway
Wallingford, CT 06492
800/PRODIGY

INTERNET LISTSERVES

VETMED-L   Send a message to
LISTSERV@UGA.CC.UGA.EDU or
LISTSERV@UGA.BITNET (for Bitnet users). In the
body of the message, say "Subscribe VETMED-L your
name."

FANCIERS' NET   Send a message to **FANCIERS-
REQUEST@AI.MIT.EDU.** In the body of the message
say, "Subscribe your name" and give a brief note
about your involvement with cats.

FELINE-L   Send a message to
LISTSERV@PSUVM.PSU.EDU or
LISTSERV@PSUVM.BITNET (for Bitnet users). In
the body of the message, say "Subscribe your name."

Answers to Quiz in Chapter 1

1. True
2. True
3. False
4. True
5. False
6. False
7. True
8. False
9. True
10. False
11. True
12. False